Intentional Interruptions is a g[...] to allow yourself to pause in yo[...] God's world, to step into some[...] and hope, and to re-connect mea[...]ly with your Lord. Reading Jonathan Thomas' book reminded me that while everyone wants a piece of me these days, the Lord wants all of me every day.

Matthew C. Mitchell
Pastor of Lanse Evangelical Free Church;
Author, *Resisting Gossip: Winning the War of the Wagging Tongue*

Jonathan Thomas has done me (and all of us!) a great favour. I'm too easily distracted by things I should be able to say no to; and not prepared enough for the divine interruptions that King Jesus puts in my path. I need strategies to counter the former; I need encouragement to see and embrace the latter. In this helpful book, Thomas has given me both.

Adrian Reynolds
Head of National Ministries, FIEC, UK

In this gem of a book, Jonathan Thomas mixes theological depth with a down to earth tone and invites us into connectivity with the Father. It is an invitation into divine interruptions, a warm rebuke to many of us who feel hooked on doing, from a humble heart, who has worn the t-shirt. This is an invitation to know God, not just know about God. To refresh our hearts before our socials, to wait on divine nudges over notifications. Thomas reminds us that rhythms don't redeem us in and of themselves, but they give us Selah moments so we can better fix our eyes on the Redeemer. Interruptions don't have to be irritating, if we give space for His divine interruptions, they can be liberating. This book has stirred me to Selah. I commend it to you.

Dai Woolridge
Spoken word poet, storyteller, and author

Inten
tional

LEARNING
TO BE

INTERRUPTED
THE WAY
Interr
uptions

GOD
INTENDED

JONATHAN THOMAS

CHRISTIAN
FOCUS

Copyright © Jonathan Thomas 2023
paperback ISBN 978-1-5271-1020-5
ebook ISBN 978-1-5271-1059-5

10 9 8 7 6 5 4 3 2 1

Published in 2023
by
Christian Focus Publications Ltd,
Geanies House, Fearn, Ross-shire,
IV20 1TW, Great Britain.
www.christianfocus.com

Cover design by Pete Barnsley

Printed and bound by
Bell and Bain, Glasgow

MIX
Paper | Supporting
responsible forestry
FSC® C007785
www.fsc.org

CONTENTS

Part 1

1. Journeying with Jesus.................................... 9

2. Just About Everyone Wants to Interrupt You............. 21

3. Jesus Wants to Interrupt You 39

4. Join the Revolution 49

5. Just Say No.. 81

Part 2

6. Creation 99

7. Compassion... 111

8. Communication....................................... 125

9. Conscience... 137

10. Communion 151

Conclusion.. 165

To Rebecca
For encouraging me to choose the right Interruptions

Part 1

1

Journeying with Jesus
A Mountaintop Interruption and the
Valley of Distraction

Thirteen of us were walking in complete silence. I could feel and hear my heartbeat. I was out of breath and every muscle in my body ached. But I felt amazing. I felt alive. I looked ahead to the six guys in front of me, backpacks laden with tents and trowels, and then back at the other six, all panting but smiling with a serenity many of us hadn't known for years. No one was saying a word, but every glance communicated more than most can say in ten minutes. We were all together, doing the same thing, having the same experience, feeling the same delight. This was a mountaintop experience.

As we started our descent, our feet clambering tiredly over white rocks in a bed of black peat bog, I was enjoying time with God. Really enjoying it. But it was strange. Usually, my quiet time is gatecrashed by emails and memes, or my prayers are hijacked by stressful thoughts and deadline reminders. Even my singing on a Sunday morning can be derailed by remembering something I haven't done. But here, now, on the side of a mountain, in the quiet, I was enjoying God. It was as if all of those usual interruptions had been interrupted.

A mountaintop Interruption

We had all agreed to come on a 24-hour hike and leave our iPads, phones and watches at home. We were completely off grid. We'd been dropped off at 10 am and had been walking ever since. No tech, no social media, no work, no distractions. Just thirteen guys hiking through the Black Mountains, learning to switch off and spend time with God. I'll be honest; it had been a struggle to convince the men to do it. A few even contacted me to ask for 'dispensation' to bring a phone ... 'just in case'. But we all ended up agreeing to it. We would leave everything behind.

Our day was led by a guide who had been a missionary in China and loved hiking in the Scottish mountains. He brought a great mix of Scripture knowledge and mountain safety. He made sure we were working through Philippians together, and that no one got lost or injured. It was as close to a Bear Grylls experience as it could get for a bunch of middle-aged men in the Welsh mountains for twenty-four hours.

It took about six hours for me to stop craving my phone, six hours not to worry about what I had missed on Twitter, six hours to start enjoying the view without stressing that I couldn't take a panoramic to post on Instagram, six hours to learn to be quiet. Our guide broke us in gently. As we walked, he instructed us to do so silently. At first, it was just for ten minutes, but I simply couldn't focus; my mind was swirling with thoughts and worries. Our guide then walked us through Philippians, encouraging us to think on the true, noble, right, pure, lovely and admirable.[1] To reflect on the creation around us and the One who created it all. The second silence was twenty minutes, and

---

1. Philippians 4:8.

I started to meditate on what we had been reading in the Bible. Now, we were going for the big silence. And I was loving it.

But then, our silence was broken by the shout of 'Water!' We had been walking for about eight hours and had used up all of our supplies. We weren't in the middle of a desert; no one was about to pass out. We knew there was a shop a couple of miles away. But to see this trickle of water coming out of the side of the mountain made us leap for joy. We were like little kids in a free sweet shop. We just couldn't get over how amazing it was to have free, clean water that had no end. We filled our bottles, lay down to rest our aching backs, and guzzled the water with glee.

I'll be honest: the experience of that physical water, cooling my lips and bringing life to my bones, was the same as the spiritual experience of the day. This day had given living water to my soul. As I sat on the grass next to the spring, sipping ice cold water from my water carrier, laughing and smiling with friends, I *felt* Psalm 23. I experienced it. I embodied it. He makes me lie down in green pastures, He leads me besides quiet streams, He restores my soul.

I was restored.

But God had more in store. His display of goodness in the beauty of creation was about to get a bonus feature. As we looked over to our right, the sun was dropping down over Pen Y Fan mountain, and it turned golden yellow and then deep red. Its rays shot out over the valleys between us, and the clouds that hung in the sky took on textures and features that no human artist could mimic. The sun was shining on my sweat-drenched face, and I could feel the Son shining on me too.

Within two hours we had reached our camp, set up our tents, and prepared some dehydrated camping food (to be honest, by that point in the day, anything would have tasted like a Michelin Star chef had cooked it). We sat around the campfire, chatted about our day and thoughts, and then started to share stories and jokes and laugh under the star-filled sky of the Brecon Beacons. Oh, and we enjoyed a nice glass of Red, from a bottle that one of the elders had secretly carried in his bag all day.

So, why did I organise to take the men of my church on such a radical walk?

Well, to understand that we need to rewind three years.

Imagine the scene …

A valley of distraction

It's 10:30 am.

I am utterly shattered.

The joy has gone.

How did I get here?

I replay the last few hours in my mind …

I woke up at 5:15 am and rolled over to pick up my phone. My screen already full of notifications: Twitter, email, Facebook, Pokemon Go (that was for my son, honest!), the list goes on. My heart rate kicks up a few gears – and that's before my usual four pre-office coffees. The reason for the change of gear in my chest was an email. One of my line managers had decided to contact me at midnight declaring that I now had three months instead of nine to complete a piece of work that would take about 100 hours. All in addition to my contracted hours.

As I held a bottle of milk and baby in one hand, and scrolled through the remnants of a Twitter spat with the other, I tried to push the pressure from my mind and focus on some good old-fashioned social media escapism. I quickly realised that an argument had erupted on the other side of the Atlantic, that involved people I didn't know, on a subject I didn't realise existed. But now I was hooked. I scrolled and scrolled, convincing myself that this was an issue I had to understand and get an opinion on.

My other boys woke up, and, as I breakfasted and dressed them, I sent a few emails, wrote a couple of posts, and started to catch up on my WhatsApp groups. Buried within the usual mix of GIFs, funny videos and adverts, there were some genuinely important and worrying messages. One friend had lost a baby, another was stressed and didn't know how to keep going, and some more work landed on my plate.

At this point, I couldn't tell if the flutters I felt in my chest were the impact of my third coffee or the swirling anxieties and concerns in my mind.

The children were ferried to childcare and then I tried to field as many calls as possible in the car, as well as take a sneaky look at my notes for the first meeting of the day in the car park. But strangely, I also felt ahead of my work. I was in this vague place where I was no longer 'living in the moment'. I was constantly thinking about the next thing – the next person. Sadly, I was no longer thinking of them as people, but rather, as deadlines and problems.

The day – in fact, life – felt like a treadmill, and I had no idea how to get off.

Is this how it is meant to be?

Some of you reading this may be struggling to understand how I let it get that bad. For others, it may not sound that bad compared with your work/life balance right now. It may be that you can see quite easily where I was going wrong and what the solutions were. I get that. I can see it too … now. Hindsight is always 20/20, and it is much easier to see the problem in someone else's life. In that season, I spent hours helping others get the speck out of their eye without the slightest sense that I was simultaneously whacking them with the plank of my own bad example.

I can identify with John Mark Comer when he writes, 'Emotionally I live with an undercurrent of a nonstop anxiety that rarely goes away, and a tinge of sadness, but mostly I just feel blaaah spiritually … empty. It's like my soul is hollow.'[2]

Do you know that feeling too?

Is this really the quality of life that Jesus died to give us? Is this truly living life to the full, in all its abundance? Honestly, when I was dredging through this season of life, intimacy with the Lord had all but disappeared. Invitations like Mark 6:31 had become ghostly: 'Come with me by yourselves to a quiet place and get some rest.'

What went wrong?

Looking back at that day, I now recognise there were two problems: hurry sickness and distraction. There was a mix of things I thought I had to do, but also things I had become addicted to. Some were imposed on me; some were self-inflicted.

In the midst of my most hurried days, I had a voice nagging in the back of my mind. It was the memory of a book I had read twenty years earlier. A little paperback that

---

2. John Mark Comer, *The Ruthless Elimination of Hurry* (London: Hodder and Stoughton, 2019), p. 2.

had a profound effect on my young Christian faith, *The Life You've Always Wanted,* by John Ortberg. It was here that I first came across the idea of 'the practice of slowing' and the phrase, 'you must ruthlessly eliminate hurry from your life.'[3] Why? Because 'hurry is the great enemy of spiritual life in our day.'[4]

The problem was, with every new stage and season of life, I kept getting hurried. First job, first house, first child, second child, third child … with each stage came a period of fresh trials and temptations. What I thought I had overcome in one stage simply morphed and blind-sided me in the next.

Two decades on from Ortberg's original observation, John Mark Comer expounds the same issue and expands it, writing: 'Pathological busyness, distraction, and restlessness are major blocks within our spiritual lives.'[5] Over the last twenty years we have moved from being busy, to being busy and distracted.

In case you haven't noticed: the world has changed beyond recognition since 2007. What happened? The dawn of the digital age.[6] The iPhone entered our lives, Facebook opened up to anyone and everyone, and Twitter started to tweet away. Within a very short time we could hold the world in our hands, and the world held us in its grip.

No longer could the worker leave emails at the office, confined to a desktop – everyone could now demand a response at any time. No longer could a pupil escape

3. John Ortberg, *The Life You've Always Wanted* (Grand Rapids: Zondervan, 1997), p. 81.

4. Ibid., p. 82.

5. Comer, p. 26.

6. There are many 'starts' to the digital age. Anything from 1950. But it seems to me that this point changed everything for everyone, in every way.

the bullying and leave it in the playground – everyone could now send messages, threats and hatred through a multiplicity of platforms, 24/7. No longer could people live in ignorant bliss of what they were missing out on – their social media made sure the FOMO (if you haven't come across that before, it means Fear Of Missing Out) was a constant companion in loneliness.

The result was, and is, that our minds have shifted focus to the intentions and expectations of others. For many, we no longer do what we want to do because we are no longer taking the time to decide what to focus on. The constant pang of stress and ping of social media gives us more than enough to focus on. This is the point that Greg McKeown makes in his book, *Essentialism*, when he declares, 'if you don't prioritise your life, someone else will.'[7] And our constantly connected lives have amplified this process to a deluge of deafening demands.

We are constantly interrupted.

And those interruptions are designed to get our attention.

No rest for the bombarded

Ultimately, these interruptions combine to take away our rest. Not just physically, but spiritually. The two are entwined. When our soul is restless, we push ourselves physically, trying to fill the void. But the converse is true too. When we get tired physically, bombarded by messages and more work, our souls become tired. To look at either in isolation is ultimately futile.

Perhaps we could call the problem of our digital age: *distracted hurry.*

---

7. Greg McKeown, *Essentialism: The Disciplined Pursuit of Less* (London: Virgin Books, UK edition, 2014), p. 10.

So, what is the answer?

Time management?

Partly, yes. But, not really.

I have read a shelf full of books about time management, rules for life, and working smarter. Many have helpful insights and tips but few of them get to the heart of the matter – the human heart.

Perhaps I can add to my definition of the issue we face: *restless, distracted hurry.*

Could it be that we can't switch off our notifications because we've become conditioned to search for rest in all the wrong places? In hurry and distraction? Have we swallowed the lie that by grasping the nettle even tighter the pain will stop? Thankfully, there is an answer. And it doesn't have to involve twenty-four hours without your phone limping over the Black Mountains, following a guide (wonderful as that was). There is One, the ultimate guide, who will meet you where you are, in whatever circumstance you find yourself, and He will give you rest.

Where are we going?

In the first half of this book, we will explore some of the interruptions that distract us, rob our attention and keep us busy. But we will dig deep and examine just why they are so addictive. What is it about interruptions that make us want to stop and keep on scrolling?

But that's not enough – the true calling of the Christian teacher is to help us see the problem, yes, but then locate it in the bigger picture. To articulate what the crisis is and then show how Christ is the answer. In order to eliminate the restlessness that drives us to distracted hurry, we must find the true rest that is only found in Christ. To do that, we need to locate ourselves in the meta-narrative of the Bible – from Genesis to Revelation, from Creation to New Creation.

But, that is *still* not enough. I don't want this to be a book that simply says do less and rest in Jesus. I think there is more to it than that. What if God wants to Interrupt us? What if He has intentions for our lives that we are missing out on due to the deliberately intentional interruptions of others? In the second half of this book, I will explore five ways in which God may want us to be Interrupted – for His Kingdom.

The aim of this book is not simply to get you off your phone, make more time to rest, or help you simplify and digitally detox. The aim is to invite you into the greatest life imaginable, one where we have the openness to be Interrupted by God and used in a way that will bring glory to Him.

Dietrich Bonhoeffer wrote, 'We must be ready to allow ourselves to be interrupted by God.'

Are you ready?

Before you read on

'It's not how many books you get through, it's how
many books get through you.'
Mortimer Adler

I find books with questions at the end of the chapters can be a help or a hindrance. But I can't figure out why. Is it the way the questions are written, or my heart when I am reading it? All I know is that I do get a lot more out of a book if I slow down, stop, and scribble. I am a self-confessed marginalia vandal.[8] I am constantly underlining, adding stars, and writing notes inside the books I read. This really helps me understand and remember what I am working through. But, and this is a big 'but', it only helps with information, not transformation. To be truly changed by what I read, I need to ponder and pray. At the end of a gripping sentence, or a chapter, I need to consider the text and close my eyes. I need to pray about it.

In the Book of Psalms, we are encouraged to do this. Actually, we are commanded to. Psalm 3 introduces a Hebrew word *Selah*. If you open your Bible you should be able to see it in verses 2, 4, and 8. Can you see it? Go on, have a look? Did you see it? You might have ... or might not have ... They are not shown in the NIV (except as a footnote), but they are in some translations like the ESV.

What does *Selah* mean?

I love the way Spurgeon sums it up:

> 'This is a musical pause; the precise meaning of which is not known. Some think it simply a rest, a pause in the music; others say it means "lift up the strain – sing more loudly – pitch the tune upon a higher key – there is nobler matter to come, therefore retune your harps". Harp strings soon get out of order and need to be screwed up again to their proper tightness, and certainly our heart-strings are evermore getting out of tune.'[9]

---

8. For the uninitiated, 'marginalia' are notes written in the margins of a text. Tony Reinke calls it 'the fine art of defacing books with pencils, pens, and highlighters'. Tony Reinke, *Lit!: A Christian Guide to Reading Books* (Crossway: Illinois, 2011) p. 147.

9. C.H.Spurgeon, *The Treasury of the Bible vol. 5* (Michigan: Baker Books, 1982), Exposition on Psalm 3.

Ultimately, it is a musical direction that shows we need to pause. We need to ponder. I love the way Alistair Begg defines it as 'think about that for a moment'. So, at the end of each chapter I will encourage us to *Selah*.

Selah

1. How would you feel about twenty-four hours without any screens or communication? Do you crave that, or fear it? Why?

2. When was the last time you had a 'mountaintop' experience with the Lord? Where were you? What led you to that moment?

3. Are you in a season of being overwhelmed by work at the moment? Do you need to talk to someone about it? Who could you share this with?

Prayer

Dear God of comfort, I am distracted and disorientated by many different pressures and priorities. I thank You that Jesus sees me with compassion, and ask that, by Your Holy Spirit, you would help me slow down, seek Your Face, and satisfy myself in You. I pray that You would interrupt me so that this valley of distraction would become a valley of vision. In the name of Jesus, Amen.

2

Just about Everyone wants to Interrupt you
Exploring and Exposing Interruptions

Whilst scrolling through Twitter the other day, the name of an old book came up. It was a paperback I bought when I was about seventeen years old and had read with a constant chuckle. *Turmoil in the Toybox* was a Christian book written to expose the dangers of Care Bears and My Little Pony, and how such cartoons could lead you into the occult. I had also been reading books by a converted witch, Doreen Irvine, at the same time, so the book looked comedic compared to her experiences.

Unfortunately, in the past, a sub-culture within Christianity became obsessed with the secret agendas of 1980s cartoons, 1970s heavy metal played backwards, and a myriad of other conspiracies. So, is my concern about tech and social media just the same? Will this book age just as badly as *Turmoil in the Toybox*? Will people reading this in 2045 laugh at my thoughts on the iPhone, Facebook and Gmail? I think that is a good question to ask. It is important to make sure that we aren't overreacting, but dealing soberly and factually with tech and social media.

So, let me begin this chapter by exploring two books that give us an insight into tech and social media that don't come from a Christian perspective. First, I'll introduce you to two

American tech insiders – guys who spent years working for the biggest social media companies, and have written about their experiences. Then, we'll have a listen to a British GP who shares about tech and social media use on Radio 4, Ted Talks, his own books, and BBC One. Only then will I spend some time looking at what some leading Christian thinkers are saying about tech and social media today.

The designer's insight

Jake Knapp and John Zeratsky wrote the New York Times bestseller *Sprint* and then *Make Time: How to Focus on What Matters Every Day*.[1] Jake worked at Google for a decade and John was a designer at YouTube and Google for nearly fifteen years. Both were product designers who helped shape some of the apps we use today. They realised that those apps (and others) interrupted them and stole their time, and so, in their desire to achieve more, they become self-coined 'time dorks' (which is the name of their newsletter about time management). They wanted to learn how to take back control of their lives – live out their own intentions, not those of others.

One of the most fascinating insights they give is how, as product designers, the apps they designed needed to become a 'default' function within a person's life. They write, 'Our phones, laptops, and televisions are filled with games, social feeds, and videos. Everything is at out fingertips, irresistible, even addictive. Every bump of friction is smoothed away.'[2] No app or feed wants to be ignored. So they have been created in order to get your attention and keep your attention quickly and easily. Think about your favourite social media sites and

1. Jake Knapp and John Zeratsky, *Make Time: How to Focus on What Matters Every Day* (London: Bantam Press, 2018).

2. Ibid., p. 5.

apps. How long does it take you to open them? Five seconds? I doubt even that.

My BBC News app notifies me of breaking news via my lock screen, even if I'm not using my phone ... it could just be lying face up on the desk next to me. Straight away, the ping and the ray of blue light catches my attention. Then, unlocking my phone with my thumb print, a microsecond to touch the notification, and I am reading the article. Three seconds. That is all it takes. Then, it leads me to see some local news I am interested in, a bit of showbiz gossip ... and ten minutes have gone. It was quick and easy. No push back, no friction, no complications, nothing.

Greg McKeown carried out research into how this worked out in different companies in his book *Effortless*.[3] He writes, 'Our brain is wired to resist what it perceives as hard and welcome what it perceives as easy. This bias is sometimes called the cognitive ease principle, or the principle of least effort. It's our tendency to take the path of least resistance to achieve what we want.'[4] It is this cognitive ease principle that product designers want to create.

The result for companies that find this simplicity is astonishing. Listen to Jake and John: 'Apple reports that people unlock their iPhones an average of eighty times per day, and a 2016 study by customer-research firm Dscout found that people touched their phones an average of 2,617 times per day. Distracted has become the new default.'[5] John shares about how he was commissioned by YouTube to try and get people to stay longer and watch more.

3. Greg McKeown, *Effortless: Make it Easier to do What Matters Most* (London: Virgin Books, 2021) p. 29.

4. Ibid.

5. Knapp, p. 80.

They redesigned the site in 2011, and, as a result, within 1 year, people were staying 60 per cent longer on the site.

We need to open our eyes and see that these technological nudges, these interruptions, are intentional. My boys interrupt me when they want me to play football, get a lift somewhere, or ask me to tell them a joke (actually, that last one isn't true ... they hate me telling dad jokes). When I am at my desk and concentrating on a task, someone knocking at the office door has an intention. They want me to stop what I am doing, and do what they want me to do. The same is true of a pop-up ad on a website or on my phone. Someone, somewhere, whether an automatic response or algorithm, wants me to focus on their product.

Why do these tech and social media companies want so much of our time? The answer is simple, 'Tech companies make money when you use their products.'[6] As they say, money makes the world go round. Or, more accurately, money makes us all sit down. But, I do think it worth quoting what they say in the next paragraph. 'Just to be clear, there's no evil empire behind it all ... they're inhabited by well-meaning nerds who want to make your days better.' Let's make sure we don't think of Google like *Turmoil in the Toybox* thought of Care Bears. Many of these apps have their place and purpose in life and society.

Yet, even if we don't believe that Mark Zuckerberg lives on a Death Star or that Steve Jobs lived in a volcano stroking a white cat, there are still problems with the addictive nature of these things. There are unintended consequences to the tactics and technologies that are deployed to distract and demand a response. Let's turn to our British GP for some reasons why.

6. Ibid., p. 87.

The medical insight

When I had to take some time off from work due to stress, a good friend who is a GP, got me to read *The Four Pillar Plan* by Dr Rangan Chatterjee.[7] It was a really helpful book at a difficult time. It encouraged me to focus on some simple tasks like learning to relax, eat healthily, sleep well and do some exercise. Whilst the book has an annoying habit of repeatedly saying that many of the good things we need have developed by cave-man needs, it is well worth plodding through. Many of his principles are ones that God has taught His people. From the need to sleep, to being grateful, so much of what Dr Chatterjee teaches is simply scriptural.

The reason for looking at this book though, is to show how a medic in the UK views tech and social media. You see, one of his top tips for living a longer, healthier life, is a *Screen-Free Sabbath*. Those are his words. As the strapline to the chapter advises, 'every Sunday, turn off your screens and live your day offline.'[8] Why should we do this? 'It's now thought that there are more mobile devices on the planet than people – truly remarkable. Some of us – me included – can find it hard to leave our e-devices alone for more than ten minutes.'[9] Okay … but what's so bad about that?

He goes on to describe how a father can't play with his son undistracted, as the constant ping of the phone demands his attention. He talks about the fact that we check work emails on our day off, and how we often open our eyes in the morning and go straight to newsfeeds and Twitter. The outcome is clear, 'This contributes to a wider problem, one that's become exponentially more problematic since the introduction of smartphones. We are finding it harder to

---

7. Dr R. Chatterjee, *The Four Pillar Plan* (London: Penguin Life, 2018).

8. Ibid., p. 36.

9. Ibid., p. 37.

switch off … Five years ago, I was convinced that the root cause of most complaints I saw in my practice was poor diet. Now, I'm convinced it is stress.'[10]

This addiction to our devices causes a stress that sends us to the GP's surgery. Could it really be that our tech and social media usage cause us to become ill? Yes it can. It is not the phone or the platform that does it, rather it is the stresses that come to us through it. And, more than that, the way it plays with our mind. Chatterjee looks at the selfie culture, and claims that 'this fires up neural pathways associated with reward and activates addiction centres in the brain such as the nucleus accumbens … My experience has been that, just like many drugs, the more you use your smartphone, the more addicted you become.'[11]

There are so many other things that apps like Instagram can affect. On a simple level, it can create FOMO (fear of missing out) and a low mood because you think everyone else is having a great time without you … or despite you. Deeper still, it can create 'perfectionist presentation' where a person tries to live up to, and create the perception of, perfection. Our chosen and suggested social media feeds a reliance on filters and un-attainable standards. Cruelly, this can lead to low self-worth, feeling inadequate, self-esteem problems, eating disorders, and depression. These are amongst the reasons why, on the doctors' orders, we should try and get our tech and social media usage under control.

Whilst there are many debates about the addictive nature of devices, the intentions of corporations, and the health implications of over-use, the possible dangers are clear. But we need to tread carefully here. We really must avoid making

---

10. Ibid.
11. Ibid., p. 38.

an inanimate object morally evil or try to attach motivations to a person, or group of people, that we don't know. So, is the iPhone evil? Is Facebook demonic? To answer that question, I want to look at a Christian who has studied both historic Christianity and contemporary culture. Someone who has experience of social media and has researched it. What does his theological reflection conclude on these matters?

The Christian insight

Tony Reinke works for *Desiring God* and has written extensively on the Christian faith and technology. One of his major contributions to our exploration is *12 Ways Your Phone Is Changing You*.[12] I love his balance in the preface when he writes, 'my phone is a window into the worthless and the worthy, the artificial and the authentic.' This resonates with me. Whilst I've bemoaned the triviality of Twitter and the enslavement of email, that is not the whole story. My phone means I can see a picture of my three-year-old enjoying craft in nursery – in real time. My Facebook account enables me to stay in contact with old friends, and see how they are doing. The apps I have that are created by missionary organisations enable me to pray for brothers and sisters around the world. I love so many things about my phone.

Reinke's aim in the book 'is simple: What is the best use of my smartphone in the flourishing of life?'[13] He digs deep to see how our phones are changing us. Each chapter explores the dangers of the smartphone: we are becoming addicted to distraction; we ignore real people in person; we become obsessed with wanting instant 'likes'; we end up lonely; lose meaning; become increasingly harsh to one another.

---

12. Tony Reinke, *12 Ways Your Phone Is Changing You* (Wheaton, Il: Crossway, 2017).

13. Ibid., p. 20.

The book is one of the best diagnostics on the subject I know of. At the end of the book, he briefly looks at 'living smartphone smart' and introduces some limits we can adopt (which I will share in Chapter 5).

Yet there is a tantalising sentence in the epilogue. A series of words that makes me hopeful. 'When we use our smartphones rightly, their shining screens radiate with the treasure of God's glory in Christ.' I am pretty sure he means more than downloading his *Desiring God* app! You see, the phone is not the enemy. Digital is not inherently dangerous. Social media is not necessarily sinful matter. Actually, we could have divine Interruptions via our screens. So, relax, this book isn't going to call you to a social media-quitting, phone-burning ceremony. Well, probably not.

Respectable sins
The deepest problem with tech and social media is not the distractions and addictions per se, but what it does to our heart. Our soul. Our inner being. On a simple (and serious) level, there is an obvious and widespread danger with tech and social media. Immorality. Anyone, anywhere, can access pornography, follow up inappropriate relationships, steal someone else's work, and a myriad of other illegal or ungodly things. Those are clear dangers that need to be avoided. But that is not the remit of this book. I want to look at a deeper, more subtle, danger. One that is often respectable. A temptation to find your satisfaction, security and status in something other than the gospel.

Deep down, we are all looking for satisfaction, status and security. We crave them and are willing to sacrifice for them. Tim Keller calls these 'counterfeit gods' in his book of the same title. He writes, 'anything can be an idol, and everything has been an idol.'[14] And I believe that tech and social media are portholes into numerous functional idols. It is not that your iPad becomes like a little Buddha that you rub the screen of for luck or a blessing. Rather, it's what our screens and social media entice us into at any and every moment. Those very things that Reinke uncovers: approval, vices, harshness, etc.

One of the most pertinent things I found in Keller's treatment of idols is the way that they offer so much, but then demand even more. The reason we get so attached to these counterfeit gods is because they deliver so well at the start. That feeling of responding to a work email on a day off, having an Instagram feed that you love scrolling through and liking, or getting a post re-tweeted by a celebrity. It feels good. It gives you status; it makes you feel secure; it offers instant satisfaction. We start off in the driving seat, we are holding the world in our hand.

Slowly, over time, however, the situation starts to change. That Saturday afternoon email feels like having a slave-master with you, you wish you could just leave your work in the office, but you know you can't. That tweet you crafted so well doesn't get any likes or re-tweets, and you start to wonder if anyone cares about what you think. The pressure of posting the perfect picture when your life is anything but perfect. Now, you are in the grip of the very things you thought you were controlling. As Keller writes, 'counterfeit gods always disappoint, and often destructively so.'[15]

This is when the real danger kicks in. These idols, these counterfeit gods, these enticing entertainments that promise so much – they start to demand from us. We start to sacrifice

---

14. Tim Keller, *Counterfeit Gods* (London: Hodder and Stoughton, 2009), p. xvi.

15. Ibid., p. xvii.

for them. All counterfeit idols are like the gods of antiquity – they demand the shedding of blood. There isn't much more heart-breaking than seeing a child looking longingly at their parent as they reply to 'just one more work email' during their pre-arranged time. That is a sacrifice too far.

How will we ever learn to stop this?

In Chapter 4, we will look at some amazing news. The most awesome message in all the world. There is a God, the only true God, who doesn't demand bloodshed from us. No, our God has shed His own blood for us. Hallelujah! That is how we are going to learn to put our screens down and enjoy quality time with our children, friends, strangers, searchers and angels (unawares).

I think the reason that we fall for the nudges that interrupt us, is because we are constantly looking for the God who creates us to know and enjoy Him. But we often find counterfeit gods, functional idols, replacements for Jesus. Let me pause there. Stop and think about that. Do you, like me, so often look for God, but in the wrong places?

Whilst I know that Jesus is enough, and that the cross has achieved everything, I often crave false assurances. As we will see, the cross means that Jesus gives us a solid security, a sonship status, and a serious satisfaction. But, whilst we live in this age of now and not-yet, there is a continual battle between the Spirit and the flesh, between the old man and the new man. This means that we often flee to our old gods, our former idols, and try to get a sense of security from always being on-call for work through our smart phone email box; or get a tangible feeling of status from the amount of Twitter followers and Instagram likes we get; and an instant satisfaction from posting a filtered, curated, image of our life on Facebook.

For some, answering an email from your phone on the sidelines of your daughter's football match on a Saturday morning represents the fact that you are the best employee and won't lose your job. In fact, the fear of losing that sense of security drives you to sacrifice that moment with your precious child. Putting a Bible verse on Instagram, with the picture of a sunset in the background, makes you look like a spiritual giant, but deep down you know you aren't sharing in delightful devotion but in a moment of desperate demand for attention and status.

Trying to be God

We can see why people want to interrupt us and how they can influence us at a heart level. But, we are not just victims of big tech and chemical reactions; there is a deeper reason why we let these interruptions become habits that write the liturgies of our hearts. As the great Reformation theologian, John Calvin wrote, our heart is a perpetual forge of idols. We seem hard wired to look to anything other than God to give us status, satisfaction and safety.

You see, we can only get distracted by these things to the degree in which we invite the nudges. I choose to buy a smart phone. I choose to sign up to social media platforms. I choose to have work email on my phone. I choose to take my phone to bed. I choose to allow notifications. I choose to prioritise the newsfeed before my Bible reading. I choose to present myself through a filter. I choose to present a polished version of my life on social media. I choose. I choose. I choose.

People and companies can only get you to buy or buy-into something that fulfils an urge, satisfies an itch, provides something we need. Tech and social media constantly interrupt us because we want them to. We need them to. We love them to. So far, we have seen that tech and social media are designed to become defaults. Companies and designers have created 'nudges' that stimulate the mind and cause repeated actions. But this is not just a simple issue of technology and biology. It isn't just that someone wants to grab our attention in order to make money, and we simply respond out of biological necessity. No, I don't think it is that simple. You see, I believe we are responsible for our own actions. That is, no tech company takes us hostage and forces us to sign up to their platforms and buy their latest upgrade. Yet, we often embrace these things with both hands, and at great cost. Because we want to.

Often the idols we seek to create aren't outside of us, but are us. Me ... you. We want to be God. This goes all the way back to the Garden. Zack Eswine picks up on this with pastoral precision in his books *Sensing Jesus* and *The Imperfect Pastor*.[16] Whilst looking at the general Christian life and church leaders in particular, I believe that the underlying temptations play out in our use of tech and social media. He lists four default settings of the fallen human heart that reveal our desire to be God.

'Everywhere for all' is the desire to be omnipresent. In social media terms, this is about FOMO. We want to be at every party, travel to every country, and be involved in every controversy. Social media gives us access to an artificial sense of this. Our phones can feel like teleportation systems from Star Trek. The problem is, in trying to be everywhere through the screen of a device, we end up not being in the

---

16. Zack Eswine, *Sensing Jesus* (Wheaton, Il: Crossway, 2013); *The Imperfect Pastor* (Wheaton, Il: Crossway, 2015).

very place we are. We no longer live in the moment – we lose our presence. The result is tragic. We miss out on the joy in front of us (family, friends, sunsets, helping those in need) and don't sit long enough to delight in the divine.

'Fix it all' is our deep longing to be omnipotent. In email and WhatsApp terms, it means always being on call, always wanting to get involved, always thinking we need to be there (virtually) because we can save the day. But we also start to self-medicate on these things. Instead of seeking the Lord when we are sad, we soak in social media. Rather than going on our knees to beg for help, we go on Google and find a fix or distraction. Often, our screens are a mirror. We may think we are looking elsewhere for help, but we are actually looking within – away from God.

'Know it all' must be the most obvious of the temptations, omniscience. We can now have access to every bit of information, both facts of science and the fate of friends. Through Wikipedia and WhatsApp we can start to think we know everything. And it is addictive. The more we know, the more we want to know. Before long, we are skim reading social media feeds to fuel our desire to feel like we know everything.

Eswine's final temptation is 'immediacy', the desire to have everything now. Patience has all but disappeared in the digital age. We no longer need to wait for a film to come to the cinema. We rarely have to endure seven days before watching the next episode of a six-part drama after a cliff-hanger. We can now binge watch it in one weekend. We have lost all sense of waiting. The entire concept of delayed gratification has been corroded with constant access to content. And this spills over into the rest of our lives. Relationships, hobbies, prayer, suffering. We don't want to wait for anything anymore, and we don't think we have to.

Can you relate to any of those temptations? Do you see any of them reflected in your life? Could your social media and tech habits be forming some of these god-like desires? It is often subtle and slow. Temptations work best in the midst of good things. Being able to know what is happening, help others in need, and get some things quickly, is good. But when those become our default setting and the ultimate aim, we have made a heart change.

The big problem with the interruptions that play with these temptations is that they can derail, not only our plans, but our hearts. Ultimately, an interruption is an invitation. But it is not an invitation to a one-off high. No, these nudges are an invitation for the heart to form new habits, liturgies and loves.

Liturgies of the soul

Many of the interruptions in our lives end up becoming regular occurrences. Something that happens a couple of times and is novel, can end up becoming a ritual … which in turn becomes a liturgy. This happens without us trying, it is part of the cognitive ease principle. No one says for a New Year's resolution, 'I am going to check Twitter every morning.' I mean, who has ever asked you to keep them accountable to make sure they have posted on Facebook every day? Very few people have to try to do those things, they just … happen. And then, they rule. One study by Duke University claims that 40 per cent of decisions are made out of habit, not choice.[17] Just think about your coffee order.

---

17. Justin Whitmel Earley, *The Common Rule* (Downer's Grove, Il: IVP USA, 2019), p. 7.

Do you choose something different every time, or just go with what you usually get? Mine's a flat-white, by the way.

But these habits, these rituals, are liturgies that form us. Let me explain.

I can still remember my first mobile phone – it was a Nokia brick, a dumb phone. I could make phone calls, send texts, and play snake. That was it. So, the occasional text would interrupt me, get my attention, and that was that. I'd only look at the phone when it vibrated or played a little tune. Fast forward twenty years and I now have a smart phone that can send me tens of alerts every hour. Facebook, Twitter, Goodreads, texts, WhatsApp, diary, WhatsApp, phone calls, WhatsApp. Okay, as you can see, especially WhatsApp groups. But, the big thing is, every time I look at the phone there is a new alert. Something has happened, and either I need to engage with it, or I am missing out.

Like some of you reading this book, I look at my phone incessantly. In fact, you may have just looked at it now. Did you? I bet you have now. The problem with this repeated habit is that the interruptions become rituals. Almost spiritual experiences. Actions that mould us, affect us, lead us and drive us. For many people, the phone is the first thing they look at in the morning, the reflex action at the hint of boredom, the soothing solution to a feeling of loneliness, the instant shot of dopamine that lifts the spirit – and that is what it is designed to do. But then it gets more powerful. You see, once the phone becomes a ritual, it takes on the power of a liturgy.

I first came across this idea in *The Common Rule* by Justin Whitmel Earley.[18] Earley shows how some habits unlock a whole host of other actions. And these habits can form the

---

18. Ibid.

heart – they are actions of formation. You see, some actions are what he calls 'keystone', 'a micro shift that brings about a macro effect.'[19] A keystone habit could be looking at your phone first thing in the morning. Many of us keep our phones plugged in at the side of our beds. It is where we set our alarms, and it is there if someone tries to contact us in an emergency … Oh, and it changes the hour automatically twice a year.

But looking at the phone first means that we end up strolling through social media first, and maybe checking our work email before we get out of bed. Those habits, or rituals, in turn speak to our heart. We are either filled with hope or fear depending on what we see. Or, we are lifted high by the re-tweets or thrust low by the pictures from the party the night before – that you weren't invited to, but everybody else seems to be having the time of their life in the Instagram pictures.

We have now set our hearts for the day. Getting out of bed the wrong way can literally be to do with the way our phone forms us. So many of the interruptions in our lives become the habits that are the architecture of our life. It is what everything is built on.[20]

Psalm 1 shows us a picture of how interruption can form us. It is the gateway to the Psalms, its manifesto. The basic premise is that there are two ways to live – the way of the wicked or the path of righteousness. Straight away, the Psalmist shows us that the way of the wicked is more 'caught' than 'taught'. We start by walking with people, then we stop to talk, and then we sit to listen and be influenced.

As I am walking along, I feel a vibration in my pocket. My heart leaps as the chemicals in my brain message me that

19. Ibid., p. 6.
20. Ibid., p. 4.

something good is coming. Like Pavlov's dog I am salivating at the anticipation of some kind of buzz. Grabbing my phone with one hand, I swipe up with the other, tap on the notification, and I'm hooked. I stop walking, standing still long enough to read something that mentions my name. Then, I see a bench, and sit down to click on the link to the message.

What Psalm 1 shows is a series of interruptions that intend to stop you hearing the voice of God. But there is good news. There is another way. The path of righteousness. It is one that changes everything, and makes us like an oak tree planted by a plentiful water source. A life that is solid – based on the status, security and satisfaction only Another can give. Another who is truly all-knowing and all-powerful. One who gave up everything for us. So it is to Him that we must turn now.

Selah

1. Have you ever noticed how websites and apps want to be friction free? One click functions? Do you tend to use those more than others?

2. How did you react to a GP advising people to have a screen Sabbath? Do you think that phones can affect our mental health? How?

3. Which of Zack Eswine's and Tim Keller's descriptions of our idolatry did you relate to?

Prayer

Heavenly Father, You are the One who sent Your only Son, the Lord Jesus, into this world as the perfect, blessed One. He delighted in Your word day and night, and followed Your ways, even to the Cross. He did that so that we could be found in Him and adopted into Your family. Help me to delight in that truth and depend on it each and every day. Help me to seek You more than anything else. In the name of our Saviour, Jesus Christ, Amen.

3

Jesus Wants to Interrupt You

Up until this point, I have been depicting interruptions as negative things. Time drains that take us away from the important things. But this is not a book on time management and personal leadership. I don't want to help you create a distraction-free life where you have more time to collect sea shells (*à la* John Piper). Rather, I want us to be freed up to live a life of Interruptions, with a capital 'I'. You see, there are *interruptions that are distractions, and Interruptions that are divine.* Here is the heart of this book: God wants to Interrupt you. Nudge you. Grab your attention. Create liturgies in your life. Not for money, but for His glory.

I believe that God wants our lives to be Interrupted.

These are deliberate, divine and designed.

Just think through some of the biggest stories in the Bible. Back in the Book of Genesis, Adam and Eve had been interrupted and distracted by the snake. The intention was clear, get them to doubt the goodness of God and then walk away from the Lord. It is the original demonstration of Psalm 1. Our parents walked with wickedness, stood to consider the way of sin, and sat down to eat in an act of defiance. As Psalm 2 continues, our original representative head said, 'Let us break their chains and throw off their shackles.'

The interruption that promised true life was actually the original lie that destroyed life.

Yet, even though we rejected our loving and lavish creator, we see an amazing and eternity-changing Interruption. Jesus walks in the garden, in the cool of the day.[1] I love the fact that this description is after the Fall! The Lord comes to speak to them, to grab their attention, to show them a better way. I like to think that He enacted a sacrifice in front of them (how else would He get their clothes of animal skin, and later be able to judge the quality of Cain and Abel's sacrifices?), and then told them all about the One who would come as the serpent crusher. This was the first divine Interruption that is the basis for all others. In grace, God comes and speaks to us, even when we have rejected His Words.

What about Noah, Abraham, Moses, Rahab, Boaz, the disciples like Simon Peter and Andrew, or the church persecutor Saul (Paul)? All of them were Interrupted by God. And these weren't just at the start of their ministries and callings, these were later on in life too. Think about how many times Abraham had divine encounters, or New Testament authors like Paul and John talk about the third heaven, or being in the Spirit on the Lord's day.

Yet we need to be careful here. We need to make sure that we don't assume that all of God's Interruptions are non-physical. That is, that God only wants to distract us from the world and the things of this world ... including its people. I guess many of us would love that. Wouldn't it

---

1. Genesis 3:8 describes the Lord God walking in the Garden; this would have been the pre-incarnate Christ.

be wonderful if divine things were only 'spiritual'? I use the term 'spiritual' because I am referring to a wrong understanding. This is an idea of 'spiritual' that forgets this world, and focuses on heaven. As a young Christian, I remember starting a Sunday service by saying, 'I don't know what kind of week you have had, but we have come to forget that, we are here to worship.' I had good intentions, but I was a functional gnostic. Then, to re-enforce my theological statement, I got us to sing a chorus that said 'and in His presence, all our problems disappear.'

Let me explain this a bit more with a famous encounter with Jesus.

Mary and Martha

As Jesus and his disciples were on their way, he came to a village where a woman named Martha opened her home to him. She had a sister called Mary, who sat at the Lord's feet listening to what he said. But Martha was distracted by all the preparations that had to be made. She came to him and asked, 'Lord, don't you care that my sister has left me to do the work by myself? Tell her to help me!'

'Martha, Martha,' the Lord answered, 'you are worried and upset about many things, but few things are needed— or indeed only one. Mary has chosen what is better, and it will not be taken away from her' (Luke 10:38-42).

Are you Mary or Martha? That may be a question you have heard a few times. But it's not the question that we should ask. Taken on its own, out of context, the passage could seem to teach that. But, read in the overall sweep of Scripture (from Creation to New Creation) and specifically in the surrounding passages, I think the passage actually teaches something quite different. Before I explain what I mean, let me share why I think this passage is so relevant for today.

Like Martha, many of us are keen to serve. And it is good to serve, especially the Lord and His priorities. I carried out a survey at my church a few years back and discovered that 86 per cent served in the congregation, and 94 per cent of those people said that it helped them mature spiritually. As the Lord Jesus said, doing the will of the Father is our food. There's loads to do in the church. In traditional set-ups we have preaching, leading, visiting, kids work and finances. In newer churches there are music bands, PA, projection, websites, and hoodies to design. All churches want to do outreach and community stuff (like foodbanks). There is loads of work in the church ... enough for everyone.

But there are always two things that make this a problem: The Pareto principle, the fact that 20 per cent of the people do 80 per cent of the work. And then, following on from that, there is fatigue over time. As the comedian Milton Jones quips, many see the church like a giant helicopter. Don't get too close, or you'll get sucked into the rotas! In church, work, families, communities, etc, there is always more to do. It is relentless. And our phones only make it worse.

Like Martha, many of us end up worrying about all that needs to be done. We start off with enthusiasm and joy, but then it turns to stress and distraction. A good thing can become an unhealthy thing. This can happen in churches. As many pastors warn their congregations: *we can be so busy doing work for God that we end up forgetting about the work of God in us.* And when that happens, we feel like Martha. Look at what she says:

'Don't you care?!'

We ask the same question: Don't You care about my ministry? Don't You care about my family? Don't You care about me and my worries? Is that you?

If so, you are not alone.

This busyness ends up in distraction, and, like Martha at times, we don't value time with God. Shockingly, Martha rebukes Jesus for letting Mary just sit at His feet and listen to Him. At this point she is missing one of the most amazing moments in history – for all human beings, but especially for women. Jesus is declaring women equal: Mary is like a disciple. Jesus has come into Martha's home, having accepted her kind invitation, but she wants to serve Jesus … at the expense of being served by Jesus.

Martha, at this point, doesn't see sitting at Jesus' feet as being important. In fact, she is annoyed by it. And that can happen to us. Our time with God disappears.

Confession

I have had days where I had so much ministry to do, that I didn't spend time reading my Bible and praying. I needed to 'get on with it'. In fact, I have had some difficult situations in my life where I have stopped praying about it, and just put more effort into it. Perhaps you have too. If you have, listen clearly. Stop feeling guilty. Look back up at the words of Jesus in verse 41.

Notice how Jesus *doesn't* respond to Martha's challenge and stress: *'Oh you little sinner, get back in the kitchen where you belong'. 'How dare you speak to me like that, go away'. 'Oh well, you're a second-rate Christian, you'll never amount to anything'.* Nope, He replies with the loving words *'Martha, Martha'.* Then He goes to the heart of the matter:

'you are worried and upset about many things'. Jesus knows what she is thinking. He knows how she is feeling.

Here is great news: Jesus knows how you are feeling. In fact, He put this passage in the Bible to help you at this time.

Then He gave her the best advice ever: Choose the better.

Now, this is where the confusion increases. Isn't Jesus saying the 'spiritual' is always better than physical? No. We need to pause, zoom out, and consider three things.

Martha did a good thing

Jesus is not saying Martha is terrible. She was the one who invited Him in. He is not saying that activity is bad. We know that because the context is the parable of the Good Samaritan! Rather, Jesus is saying that it is 'better' – 'the best thing' – 'the important thing' to sit at Jesus' feet. This is about the priority of time with God in order to live a life for God. Priority, not exclusivity.

The context to this passage is Jesus sending out the seventy-two in Chapter 10. Then making sure that they have a rounded ministry that involves making sure their hope is in the gospel, not their ministry; doing all the good they can; but not neglect time with God, which is shown here as resting in the gospel, and in the next section, learning to pray. Look at how the section works:

- Jesus sends us all out on a mission: Great Commission

- Jesus wants us all to rest in the gospel: Who we are in Christ

- Jesus wants us all to do good: spiritual and physical/ mission and mercy

- Jesus wants us all to spend time with Him, in the Word and prayer

Spurgeon says in his sermon on this passage:

> It is not an easy thing to maintain the balance of our spiritual life. No man can be spiritually healthy who does not meditate and commune; no man, on the other hand, is as he should be unless he is active and diligent in holy service.[2]

As you will see in the second half of this book, I think God wants to Interrupt us in many different ways, and some of those include physical, practical moments and ministries. Think about Rahab being Interrupted to help the Israelites, Boaz leaving the edges of his fields for gleaning, and Jesus consistently responding to non-diarized meetings. The Samaritan woman at the well, the woman who had been bleeding for years, the short tax collector hanging out of a tree, or the thief on the cross asking to be remembered. Jesus was open to Interruptions. They were divine, not distractions. As we will see in Chapter 7, we can be like the Priest and Levite on the road from Jerusalem to Jericho, ignoring the need in front of us for 'spiritual' reasons.

We need to find this balance that Spurgeon speaks of. But, we need to understand that this balance is not of two equal parts. There is a primacy, a best, a better, an essential first. That is what Mary chose. You see, our problem is that we go and do, but we don't sit and be, and then we end up distracted, worried and upset. We end up like Martha. This passage is not condemning work – it is good. But it is not the better. And without the better, work becomes a cruel taskmaster.

---

2. Spurgeon, p. 803.

Mary did a better thing

Kent Hughes writes that 'the story of Mary and Martha is actually about the necessity of the priority of the word of God in the life of active service for the master'.[3] This is not contemplation versus activity. This is about the need to spend time with God in order to serve Him. Alistair Begg once said in a sermon I heard that Jesus is saying, 'I want to talk to you about the quality of your relationship with me, rather than the quantity of your work for me.'

We need to realise that prayer and Bible study are key. That is what we tend to skip. We try and do the work of God without God. Time alone with God brings focus. We get the bigger picture. Everything is put back into scale, the scale of God. That is why it is the better thing. Let Jesus serve you.

So, who are you? Martha or Mary? That is the standard application. But that is not the point. I think we need to be both. For neither is the hero of the story, nor the answer to our distracted hurry sickness. This book is not about being the perfect Mary, or a more efficient Martha. No, this book is about the real hero of the story.

Jesus is the real hero of the story: the better

Look back at the passage. God is here. He is speaking. He is empowering. He is comforting. God is speaking through His Word ... the Word! And Jesus is speaking to you today, through His Word (let me be clear, I don't mean my book). The passage is not saying: don't work and be a Martha, rather just sit and be a Mary. No, the Holy Spirit is saying, come to Jesus, listen to Him! Which is how this section in Luke was set up in the Transfiguration. We need to listen to Jesus.

---

3. Kent Hughes, *Preaching the Word: Luke Vol. 1* (Wheaton, Il: Crossway, 1998), p. 395.

At this point, many of us moan. We think that because we don't live in the time of Jesus, we can't be Mary and sit at His feet. Jesus is in heaven. Dare I say, many of us feel worse off than the believers in the times of the Gospels. But that is a mistake. It is a theological slip. Actually, I believe we are in a better position. Better than Mary? Yes! We live post-Pentecost and so now we can enjoy communion with God, through the Holy Spirit, who dwells within us. Union with Christ means that I am in Christ and He is in me. I am His, and He is mine. All the time.

Wonderfully, Bible reading is not an intellectual exercise but a means of grace. The Spirit who inspired the text is also able to illuminate our hearts and minds when we read it. We can be like the disciples on the road to Emmaus and feel our hearts burn within us. For the Christian today, we find Christ in the Word, but Christ is in us by His Spirit, and so to read the Bible in a prayerful manner is to meet with Christ. It is communion. It is a means of grace. We don't merely learn about Jesus, rather we meet with Jesus – intimately.

We should desire this. We should be desperate for this. We should make time for this … prioritise it. Ann Griffiths, a Welsh hymn writer, longed to spend time with Jesus and wrote:

> Oh, that we may spend our days
> In a life of exalting his blood;
> Hiding quietly under his shadow,
> Living and dying at his feet;
> Carrying the cross, and continuing to lift it,
> Since it is the cross of my Own one,
> Finding my interest in his person,
> And worshipping him, my GOD.[4]

---

4. John Ryan, *The Hymns of Ann Griffiths*, (Y Llyfrfa: Caernarfon, 1980) p.133

Selah

1. What has stood out to you in this chapter? Why?

2. Are you a Martha? How?

3. Are you asking: 'don't you care?' Why?

4. When was the last time you sat down and listened to God?

Prayer

Dear Jesus, I long to sit at Your feet and hear Your voice. Forgive me for being distracted and worried about many things, from scrolling, social media and stress. I thank You that You call my name in grace and invite me to rest in You. Help me to listen to You, sit at Your feet, and follow You. In the precious name of Jesus, Amen.

4

Join the Revolution
Seeing how our identity changes everything

During my time at university I was in a cover band called Balaam's Donkey that played a mix of The Beatles, Chesney Hawkes and Delirious? (you had to be there). Over the years, we've got together to play weddings and birthday parties with a guilty-pleasure nostalgia that only makes sense if you were a student in the '90s. A little while ago, we played for a birthday party in Warwick. It was a great evening, but after a long Saturday I was desperate to get home to sleep before my sermon the next morning. And so, without realising, I drove in the wrong direction.

I thought that home was south, when, in fact, it was west. The faster I went, the further away from home I drove. It took me a couple of hours to realise that London wasn't close to Abergavenny, and that I better turn around.

If you find yourself in my shoes and are going in the wrong direction, it doesn't matter how hard you work and try – things will only get worse. So, let's stop and take our bearings – check the map – find out how to swap our lower-case interruptions for the better, divine, upper-case Interruptions. To do this, we will go to the heart of the matter and explore our identity: who we are. This can help us to start heading in the right direction.

Two sets of three alliterations

Over the last few years I have tried to formulate a simple way to get on top of my social media and stress. Instead of finding the one silver bullet, or the top ten actions, I have come up with two sets of three alliterations that I think are faithful to the Bible, and helpful in getting on top of work and the web.

In this chapter, we will explore three 'C's that place our identity in the meta-narrative of the Bible. That is, the big picture of who God has made us to be, and how we should orientate ourselves in the universe. This bigger picture will define us. It is very simple to remember: creation, cross and consummation. The only word that might seem strange is 'consummation'. Basically, I am using that to talk about the Lord Jesus' Second Coming and the eternity we all face – when everything is made right. But within that framework, we will look at three things that God commands us to do, three small words that will direct us: sleep, Sabbath and slowing. The third concept could also be Selah (which we have explored already), or stopping.

So, now you know the direction we are going, and hopefully it isn't the wrong way like that fateful drive home. Let's explore …

C1: Creation

Let's go back to the beginning of humanity and consider how and why God made us. Genesis tells us that God created everything out of nothing, as Graham Kendrick poetically sings, with 'hands that flung stars into space.' It is an awe-inspiring thought. Let's pause and consider Psalm 8 here.

Lord, our Lord,
how majestic is your name in all the earth!
You have set your glory in the heavens.
Through the praise of children and infants
you have established a stronghold against your enemies,
to silence the foe and the avenger.
When I consider your heavens,
the work of your fingers,
the moon and the stars,
which you have set in place,
what is mankind that you are mindful of them,
human beings that you care for them?
You have made them a little lower than the angels
and crowned them with glory and honor.
You made them rulers over the works of your hands;
you put everything under their feet:
all flocks and herds,
and the animals of the wild,
the birds in the sky,
and the fish in the sea,
all that swim the paths of the seas.
Lord, our Lord,
how majestic is your name in all the earth!

I live on the edge of the Brecon Beacons, the first International Dark-Sky reserve. One website says that

> 'on a clear night in the Brecon Beacons, you can see the Milky Way, major constellations, bright nebulas and even meteor showers. It's enough to make anyone starry eyed. Our Park has some of the highest quality dark skies in the whole of the UK, making it the perfect destination for stargazers.'

Gazing at the stars is amazing … they make us stand back in awe at our creator God. It's amazing that God made the stars and sustains them (every single one – all 100 octillion!).

But, having seen the majesty of God in the wonder of creation, we are then meant to marvel at the way He has created us … and cares for us. We are tiny compared to the cosmos, yet humankind is the pinnacle of the creation account in Genesis. This is a truth that should fill us with wonder and worship and make us truly starry-eyed. We are meant to cry out, 'Who are we? Why do You care about us?'

We are divine image-bearers
Everything was good in creation before we set foot on the earth. And then, when God created humanity together, it was very good. One reason for this is because we were created in the image of God, to represent Him on earth and have a relationship with Him.

Just pause there …

A relationship! We can know God. He wants to know us. God has created us with a spiritual capacity, an ability to know and be known. We can feel puny – tiny – insignificant, especially compared to the stars in the night sky. But to God, we are not insignificant. He cares for us and wants us to know Him. Look up at verse 5: He crowns us with glory.

But, before we get carried away with our crown, we need to look down and remember that we came from the ground.

We are dust
In his powerful little book *Zeal Without Burnout,*[1] Christopher Ash writes about having come 'at least twice

---

1. Christopher Ash, *Zeal Without Burnout* (Epsom: The Good Book Company, 2016).

… to the edge of burnout,'[2] and goes on to explore how that made him realise that we need to remember the neglected truth that we are creatures of dust. We see this clearly in Genesis 2:7. I love the honesty and pastoral helpfulness in his statement, 'I am frail and fragile, and I do well never to forget it.'[3]

The temptation has always been to forget our frailty. To ignore the fact that we are dust. Smart phones and social media perpetuate that lie by making us think we can be all-knowing, in all places, at all times. Moreover, because most people present themselves through filters and edited highlights, we start to think that everyone else is more than dust … and that we should be too.

But God didn't want us to believe that. He wants us to know our limitations, our frailty. And that is a wonderfully freeing feeling. We don't have to do all the things all the time. Being able to understand our personal limits is actually a sign of strength. We don't have to push ourselves beyond our limits.

Before we move on the C2, the cross, let's look at the three S's that come out of the fact that we are created beings. These are ways in which God designs us to remember and realise our limitations: sleep, Sabbath and slowing. As we will see, we shouldn't let our life be led by algorithms, but by these three ultimate rhythms of creation.

S1: Sleep

Let me point out an obvious observation that needs careful consideration. God designed us to sleep, before the Fall. Think about that. In the beginning, when Adam and Eve

---

2. Ibid., p. 15.
3. Ibid, p. 40.

were created, when they were very good, they were made to sleep. It is part of the original design brief of human beings. Our bodies, even in their pre-Fallen state, were masterfully made to sleep. Sleep is good. Sleep has a purpose. As Adrian Reynolds says, 'Sleep is part of our created humanity, a good gift from God to be treasured and enjoyed.'[4] Yet, we take our smart phones to bed and cause a sleep-deprived danger zone that is contrary to the creator's care.

According to one study done in 2011, only 38 per cent of people are classified as 'good sleepers'.[5] An extraordinary 36 per cent were classified as having possible chronic insomnia, a condition which involves serious sleep deprivation 'for a period of four weeks or more'. Sleep is a struggle for many, but it would seem to me that this problem has only been made worse, over the last decade, by social media and smart phones. From my own experience, I know that using a phone in bed will stop me falling to sleep. The little light and the tantalising tweets make me stay awake longer, in a strange stupor that is neither energised not energising. It is just meh. Dr Chatterjee explains the science behind the problem:

One of the worst things you can do in the hour or two before bed is look at your smartphone or tablet. Believe it or not, these electronic devices emit the same wavelength of light as the morning sun. Confusingly it's called 'blue light', and just by looking at our phones, we're duping our bodies into thinking it's the start of the day.[6]

---

4. Adrian Reynolds, *And So To Bed* (Ross-Shire: Christian Focus Publications, 2014), 10.

5. Ibid.

6. Chaterjee, p. 216.

The UK's Mental Health Foundation is clear. 'Sleep is as important to our bodies as eating, drinking and breathing, and is vital for maintaining good mental and physical health. Sleeping helps to repair and restore our brains and our bodies'. Sleep is a gift from God that we reject at our peril.

Here is the big question: why did God design us to need sleep? He didn't have to. He could have created us in any way He wanted to. But He wanted us to sleep, to rest, to close our eyes. Sleep, by God's design, is a daily reminder that we are but dust, with limitations. It is a cyclical moment where we must close our eyes and admit that we are no longer needed. In fact, if you don't sleep, you will make yourself very ill. Sleep deprivation is a form of torture.

Sleepy Psalms

What is your bedtime like? Horlicks and happiness? Soap operas and suppression of sadness? Wine and wallowing? Sleeplessness and sorrow? We can reclaim a better evening ritual with a theology of bedtime. In fact, the third and fourth Psalms can help us do this. They work as a pair. Psalm 3 is a morning prayer, and Psalm 4 is an evening prayer. Have a little look at Psalm 4 with me:

> Answer me when I call to you,
> my righteous God.
> Give me relief from my distress;
> have mercy on me and hear my prayer.
> How long will you people turn my glory into shame?
> How long will you love delusions and seek false gods?
> *Selah*
> Know that the Lord has set apart his faithful servant
> for himself;
> the Lord hears when I call to him.
> Tremble and do not sin;

when you are on your beds,
search your hearts and be silent.
Selah
Offer the sacrifices of the righteous
and trust in the Lord.
Many, Lord, are asking, 'Who will bring us prosperity?'
Let the light of your face shine on us.
Fill my heart with joy
when their grain and new wine abound
In peace I will lie down and sleep,
for you alone,
Lord, make me dwell in safety.

I wonder, when it comes to sleep, how many of us would like to be able to say, 'In peace I will lie down and sleep'? Yet, Psalm 4 doesn't start with this. Whilst this should be the experience of all believers at all times, it is not. According to the Psalm, we have to go on a journey (in the right direction) to get there.

The psalmist is experiencing something many of us can identify with – a bedtime when our heads gush with a deluge of thoughts: *I haven't done something I was meant to do; I have done something I wasn't meant to do; There is nothing else I can do … it is too late; They have done something they shouldn't have; They haven't done something they should have.* And, in our culture, the ping of the phone at dusk can be the trigger that leads to a pang of the heart and mind. But these pressures are nothing new, and, like the psalmist, many of us come to the end of our day feeling weary and worried.

So, what do we do about this?
We need to realise that bedtime is always a decision time. Our default setting is to **do**. That is, we are always trying to be in control. And often we are – or at least think we are.

But the end of the day is designed by God for a reason. Listen to Eugene Peterson:

> Psalm 4 marks the transition from the daylight world, in which it is easy to suppose that we are in control, to the night world in which we relinquish our grip on jobs, people, even thoughts.[7]

We are physically forced to spiritually reflect and rest. It is time to give up control – to stop trying to be king. Bedtime is always decision time: Will we rest or not? Will we give everything over to God or not? And our handsets are a keystone habit that can push us to create liturgies that bring us to the brink of exhaustion.

Zack Eswine writes:

> One purpose for our bed in the night is to ponder in our hearts what troubles us and to speak such things to God … Sleep is a gift, a discipline, and sometimes a luxury. As a gift it provides for our limits. As a discipline it humbles us to admit to everyone that we are finite and must stop for a while … Sleep is meant for our refreshment and strength.[8]

It can be tempting to numb our thoughts and minds through screen time rather than prayer time. We need to learn to take things to God. Not our screens.

We can reset bedtime to be a ritual to remember creation – that we are but dust and we need to sleep. But it is also a time to remember the cross – we are beloved (as we will see below). By doing this every day, we reset our default setting and train ourselves to know our true identity. This will have

---

7. Eugene Peterson, *Answering God* (New York: Harper One, 1991), p. 62.
8. Eswine, Location 1184..

a profound and powerful impact on the interruptions that we allow to direct our days.

But what about those nights when sleep evades us, when the busyness of the working day or family concerns have wired our brains? Actually, what should we do every night? Call out to a Holy and merciful God (v. 1). It is our view of the character of God that determines our sleep patterns. Then we have a Selah – a time to ponder your heart in bed. Did you see the movement in the Psalm? We go from calling out to silence … Selah. There is a time to speak and there is a time to be silent. We need to follow that order … speak, then silence.

We live in a society where we have TVs in our bedroom or iPads on our laps – and so we can't 'search our hearts and be silent.' This is one of the reasons why we wake up so tired. That's why we don't have energy to say 'no'. This is why we can miss the Interruptions that God has for us. If we don't spend time searching our hearts, then even in sleep we will still be running from God. David assumes the Selah will lead to silence and refreshing sleep.

S2: Sabbath

The second creation principle that we need to look at is the Sabbath. But, unlike sleep, this one is optional. We are not forced by physical necessity to do it every day; rather, we are commanded (and blessed) to do it each week. Back in creation, although God didn't need to take a day off, He did. His day of rest was designed to put a rhythm into the week that all of us would follow. He is the only one who doesn't need a day off. But He did it anyway. He did it for us. As always, Ash gets to the heart of the matter when he writes that if we neglect to Sabbath, 'we are implicitly claiming an affinity with God that mortals cannot have.'[9]

Over the years, the idea of a Sabbath, a day of rest, or a day for church, has been met with a variety of responses. Some have seen it as a day to fill with as much church as possible. A day when all sports, shops and socialising (outside of official fellowship) is banned. No one set out to make it like that, but the formal nature of the oral traditions added to the creation command, naturally made it legalistic.

For others, the pendulum has swung and now there is no such thing as a Sabbath. We have seen the blessing as a burden, and so feel that the Sabbath should be shelved. Often, this is an unintended consequence of pushing against legalism. But, surely, this is a law to liberate. We can see that we can't work every day of the week and still flourish physically, psychologically and as a family. It is good to have time off from work, it is good to do something different from the normal. And so, many are reclaiming this wonderful idea of a Sabbath.

John Mark Comer encourages a weekly Sabbath by defining it as 'a day to stop: stop working, stop wanting, stop worrying, just stop.' Don't we all want that? But it is a big step of faith to do that. Kevin DeYoung says that God offers us a Sabbath as 'an opportunity to trust God's work more than our own.'[10] Just like sleep, it is an opportunity to let God be God.

When we stop and consider our creation, we can clearly see that we have limitations. But these are all complicated and compounded by the Curse. This is the result of the Fall. Having rejected God and gone our own way, deciding we

---

9. Ash, p. 57.
10. Kevin DeYoung, *Crazy Busy* (Downer's Grove, IVP, 2013), p. 92.

knew best, we have been cursed. From Genesis 3, we see that life will be hard: work will be toil, and we will know the sweat of our brow. We are meant to struggle with work. It is meant to be hard. Our bodies get older and frailer. Then we are meant to ache and yearn for something more. Rest. God then gives us a Sabbath to show us that there is a Great Sabbath, a deeper rest, an eternal enjoyment.

Sabbath is about rest. Holy rest. A divine Interruption to our week, to reset our heart, and help us remember our creator, the cross and the consummation of it all in heaven. For that to happen, we need to get into a regular habit that creates a liturgy of grace. Adam Mabry is helpful when he says 'biblical rest is less rule and more rhythm – less curmudgeonly restriction and more liberating art form. It is something to be embraced and enjoyed.'[11]

My church community group was thinking through the Sabbath principle one evening. As it was during the exit of a lockdown, we were easing into meetings and so met outside. Sitting in a garden, we came to the conclusion that to enjoy a Sabbath today we would need to stop consuming and producing. That is, try and get off the treadmill of striving to achieve our status, security and satisfaction in anything other than the gospel. And then, instead of having an empty day of nothing, we should replace consuming and producing with church and creativity. That is, enjoy God's people and His gospel, and then learn to create things rather than consume them. That could be art, music, gardening, making family memories, or simply walking and enjoying creation. The Sabbath can be a day that is completely different from every other day. Rest.

---

11. Adam Mabry, *The Art of Rest* (Epsom: The Good Book Company, 2019), p. 19.

In his book *Soul Rest*, Curtis Zackery writes, 'One of the most fundamental things that we can discover in our pursuance of God throughout the Scriptures is His desire for humanity to understand Sabbath and experience rest.'[12] Surely, as we will see practically in the next chapter, a vital part of resetting our hearts is re-learning the joy of Sabbath. This must be one of the loveliest gifts that God has given us.

Yet few of us are enjoying a weekly Sabbath. I'll be honest; I struggle with it. As Justin Whitmel Earley writes in *The Common Rule*, 'the very idea of taking a day off is at best quaint and at worst scandalous.'[13] In the past, I have convinced myself that everyone is watching and judging me. To take a day off seemed impossible and unethical.

S3: Slow (*Selah*, Stop)

This is one of the central beats of this book. I am continually circling back to it. From the opening chapter where I shared about the need to ruthlessly eliminate hurry from our lives, to the exploration of sleep and Sabbath here, and later the divine Interruption of communion with God. The need to slow down, *Selah* and stop, is first in the process of getting our lives back, and it is part of the aim. Whilst we may live busy lives for the glory of God, we need never endure hurried lives for the demands of others. Jesus wants to free us from that.

The American Christian influencer (if there is a such a thing), Jefferson Bethke, has an interesting way of explaining and exploring this concept. I like the way he frames slowing: 'To follow Jesus we need to not just follow his teaching, but also his way. His process. His cadence. His demeanour. His Spirit. His very essence.'[14] I love that. But

---

12. Curtis Zackery, *Soul Rest* (Bellingham: Kirkdale Press, 2018), p. 3.
13. Earley, p.146.
14. Jefferson Bethke, *To Hell with the Hustle: Reclaiming your Life in an*

to do that, we need to get to know Jesus. We need to read the Gospels, dig deep into what He does, what He says, how He reacts, and see what He spends His time doing. Books like *Gently and Lowly* by Dane Ortlund give us a wonderful window into the heart of Jesus.

The concept of slowing is about creating space. Everything beautiful has room. Think about music. It's the rests between notes, variations in instruments played, and spaces to breathe, that help create a symphony that lifts your heart. Or consider architecture. It's the windows, open spaces, light and air that transform a building from a dark box into a living home. We need those spaces in life.

Jesus made sure that there was space in His life. Not just sleep every day, and Sabbath every week, but a daily slowing. There were times in His day, no matter how crazy the crowds or deep the desperation of those around Him, when He slowed down. And sometimes He stopped.

When He was struggling through the crowds, with shouts and jeers all around, He slowed down to find out who touched the hem of His garment, to talk to a little man climbing up a tree, and to go and spend time with dear grieving sisters. His pace wasn't perpetual. But His cadence was consistent. He would seek and serve the lost with great passion, but then He would take time out to pray to His Father.

John Mark Comer looks at how Jesus would seek out *eremos*. This is the Greek word behind places like desert, deserted place, desolate place, solitary place, lonely place, quiet place, wilderness.[15] We see this *eremos* coming up when Jesus rises early in the morning to go and pray. Whilst

---

Overworked, Overspent and Overconnected World (Nashville, Thomas Nelson, 2019), p. 4.

15. That list is taken from Comer, pp. 123-124.

I can't find a rule in the life of Jesus that says He did it every day at the same time, there is certainly a rhythm to it. It is part of His cadence. And it was something He encouraged the disciples to do. Go and pray, go and sail, go and get some food, come and rest. It's a rhythm you can feel.

But, at times (actually, a lot of times), this was a difficult time to defend. Look at this day in the life of Jesus and His disciples in Mark 6:

Then, because so many people were coming and going that they did not even have a chance to eat, he said to them, 'Come with me by yourselves to a quiet place and get some rest.'

So they went away by themselves in a boat to a solitary place. But many who saw them leaving recognized them and ran on foot from all the towns and got there ahead of them. When Jesus landed and saw a large crowd, he had compassion on them, because they were like sheep without a shepherd. So he began teaching them many things.

By this time it was late in the day, so his disciples came to him. 'This is a remote place,' they said, 'and it's already very late. Send the people away so that they can go to the surrounding countryside and villages and buy themselves something to eat.'

But he answered, 'You give them something to eat.'They said to him, 'That would take more than half a year's wages! Are we to go and spend that much on bread and give it to them to eat?'

'How many loaves do you have?' he asked. 'Go and see.' When they found out, they said, 'Five—and two fish.'Then Jesus directed them to have all the people sit down in groups on the green grass. So they sat down in groups of hundreds and fifties. Taking the five loaves and the two fish and looking up to heaven, he gave thanks and broke the loaves. Then he gave them to his disciples to distribute to the people. He also divided the two fish among them all. They all ate and were satisfied, and the disciples picked up twelve basketfuls of broken pieces of bread and fish. The number of the men who had eaten was five thousand.

Immediately Jesus made his disciples get into the boat and go on ahead of him to Bethsaida, while he dismissed the crowd. After leaving them, he went up on a mountainside to pray.

Later that night, the boat was in the middle of the lake, and he was alone on land. He saw the disciples straining at the oars, because the wind was against them. Shortly before dawn he went out to them, walking on the lake. He was about to pass by them, but when they saw him walking on the lake, they thought he was a ghost. They cried out, because they all saw him and were terrified.

Immediately he spoke to them and said, 'Take courage! It is I. Don't be afraid.' Then he climbed into the boat with them, and the wind died down. They were completely amazed, for they had not understood about the loaves; their hearts were hardened.

When they had crossed over, they landed at Gennesaret and anchored there. As soon as they got out of the boat, people recognized Jesus. They ran throughout that whole region and carried the sick on mats to wherever they heard he was. And wherever he went—into villages, towns or countryside—they placed the sick in the marketplaces. They begged him to let them touch even the edge of his cloak, and all who touched it were healed.

As I have written elsewhere, we all need to hear the wonderful word of Jesus in verse 31, 'Come'. And look at how this 'come' is expanded here. Come with me ... by yourselves. Jesus Himself is our rest. But, I don't want you to get this verse out of context. Life was hectic and hard at this time.

Crushed by the pressure

John the Baptist has just been beheaded, and so Jesus must have been emotionally drained. But there was so much work to do that He and the disciples didn't even have time to eat. They must have been physically drained too. We need to understand that Jesus was fully man, and that He experienced all of our strains and stresses. He can sympathise with us because He is one of us. But Jesus knew that this was not sustainable, and so He commanded the disciples to rest – with and in Him. And so, in verse 32, He invites them to the *eremos*.

This is so simple. When you get overwhelmed, get out of the pressure. Rest in Jesus.

Okay, before you throw this book across the room, shouting, 'It isn't that easy!', let me admit something. I know it isn't that easy. I know it isn't simple. Life is complicated. Life is messy. And we see that in the passage. Let's get back to it.

Complications of life

In verse 33, the people don't see the disciples' need for rest; they just see their own need for food. Sacrificially, Jesus sees their needs and makes a judgement call, and decides to feed them. Understandably, the disciples see a big catering problem coming and so they decide to send the people away – avoid the hard command of Jesus. Were they right to do that? Isn't this a book about stopping and serving yourself? No. No it's not. Sometimes, as we will see in the second half of this book, the upper-case Interruptions are the needs of compassion or opportunities to communicate the good news of Jesus.

Notice what is happening here. Jesus commands them to work when they should be resting. But He empowers them to do it. He performs a miracle in their time of weakness, He multiplies the food. Dear reader, in all of this talk of frailty and fallenness, slowing and stopping, we must never forget that the Holy Spirit dwells within us, and (at times) we can do far more than is humanly possible.

But that doesn't mean that we should carry on in a constant state of crushing exhaustion.

Command re-pursued

Whilst Jesus commands the disciples to miss some slowing in order to serve others, we need to realise that this was a divine Interruption. The art of Christian living is knowing when that is. Not every interruption is from God. But the key thing to notice is that, after this Jesus makes them go on a boat to get away from it all, and Jesus Himself goes to pray. In the end, we have to slow down.

Okay, all is sorted … there is now time for rest and refreshment. Yes? No! A storm comes, and now they are straining at the oars.

I love this passage. It feels like a Friday afternoon in ministry. I am nearly finished with my sermon prep, and ready to wind down to spend some time with the family, but then a pastoral emergency erupts, the car breaks down, and my computer crashes. Argh!

Perhaps you know the Sunday morning dance to get to church with three young children. Everyone is up in time, and you are excited to get the children to Sunday school. It's all working well until one of your little angels throws a tantrum, another throws a toy, and you have to throw your schedule out of the window. Slowing down is often a nightmare to achieve. I know. Trust me. This book has taken a year longer to write than I anticipated.

Calming the storm

But all is not lost. Just as Jesus performed a miracle to feed others, He now does one to calm the storm. To feed the disciples spiritually. He gives them a supernatural rest, and He teaches them, and us, through it: we need to trust Him for rest, even in the storms of life. The result is that they can crack on and carry out more ministry. Again, dear reader, please realise that this book is not simply some top tips or practical pointers to living a more time-efficient life. A lot of these ordinary means that I recommend can have extraordinary measure with Jesus.

The question is, are we willing to struggle to stop?

We can't sleep, we fear slowing down, and we won't Sabbath

Tim Chester is someone who has a great gift at exploring the human heart and applying the gospel with precision. In his book *The Busy Christian's Guide to Busyness*[16] he highlights six heart motivations that stop us slowing down and stopping. As he says, 'Do you ever think your busyness is inevitable, unavoidable or appropriate? I want to suggest that it may be none of those things. It may be that your heart is deceiving you.' Wow! Let's walk through the six heart desires he highlights.

Firstly, some us are busy because we feel the need to prove ourselves. In the community where I live, we often introduce and define people by their job titles. We live in

---

16. Tim Chester, *The Busy Christian's Guide to Busyness* (London: IVP, 2008).

a society where *what we do* determines *who we are*. Our worth is directly linked to our work. So, we work harder, and strive for success, whatever the cost, because we feel the need to prove ourselves.

Secondly, some of us are busy because we let the expectations of others set our agendas (although not every personality type functions like this). The idea of letting someone down, or losing face, is terrifying. We want to be people of our word – reliable and well thought of. This means that when someone asks us to do something, we say 'yes', even though that extra responsibility may take us away from something far more important. Ironically, sometimes putting us into a position where we let someone else down.

Thirdly, we can be busy because things get out of control. This builds on the first two heart issues. Once we start seeking work to give us status, and then accept work from others to make us pleasing, work piles up. In the end, it becomes unmanageable, and we start to drop some of the plates we are spinning.

Fourthly, some of us are busy because we actually like being under pressure. I'll pause here and be honest. I like pressure. I like feeling wanted and needed. I like the buzz. I remember driving a famous evangelist across Wales to get between meetings. I could see he was tired, and he asked to listen to himself preach on the car stereo, so he could prepare his message. I was amazed that he was so busy, that this was the only prep time he had. Then he turned to me and said, 'Brother, I love this.' He loved the pressure. Do you? I know I do, and it is toxic.

Fifthly, we are busy because we want more. We can experience internal and external pressure to succeed and see our worth in what we produce. Please hear me, I understand that some have no choice but to work three jobs in order to put food on the table. What I am writing about here are those who earn more than enough to live on, but feel the pressure to work extra hours to get a third car, fourth holiday, or bigger barn to keep all their worldly wealth in.

Sixthly, we are busy because we want to make the most of this life. Ultimately we all have some sort of 'bucket list' – even if it isn't written down. There is so much to enjoy and explore in this life. We want to live life to the full. Social media now makes this even more tantalising as we watch influencers and friends go to places we've never been or decorate their homes in ways that would make a great TikTok reveal. The ache of FOMO drives us to be more and more busy.

All of these come from the Fall and our obsession with being God, or simply ignoring Him. We are looking for our security, status and satisfaction in all the wrong places. But, if we can remember that we are dust, and that we are derailed, and then start to slow down, sleep and Sabbath, we will realise (and relish!) that the answer to our problems does not reside with us. We can slow down, stop, sleep, Sabbath and slay the social media sinkhole. But to do this, we must look outside of ourselves, to the One who is neither frail nor fallen.

Let's go back to Psalm 8 to explore our identity a bit more.

He loves 'our feeble frame'

Even though we who are from dust have feeble frames, the Lord loves us. Look at the way David picks up on the amazing claim that we have been crowned in glory. We truly are the pinnacle of creation. But the description of our position is slightly strange. He says that we are rulers, and that everything is under our feet. Really?

I can't get a cat to obey me, let alone all the animals in the world. One of the results of the Fall is that we are out of kilter with the creation. And David knew that too. Not everything is under our feet. John Stott helps us to understand what David is teaching when he states that 'Humankind has sinned and fallen, and consequently has lost some of the dominion which God has given us; but in Jesus, the second Adam, this dominion has been restored.'[17] .

That is what David meant. You see, whilst he was talking about us, he then looked to the Ultimate Human – the Second Adam – the True Human. Jesus. Psalm 8 isn't primarily about us. No, the fish don't obey me! Rather, this is about Jesus. And when I see Him, the Psalm will make much more sense. You can check out the New Testament making this very point in Hebrews 2:6-9 and 1 Corinthians 15:25-27.

This is amazing. The God who created the stars cares for us. But more than that – after we gave it all away in the Fall – He came to us. He became one of us. And in dying for us, He brought us back into relationship with Him, each other, and the creation. And part of that must surely be reclaiming sleep, Sabbath and slowing. The cross means that we can redeem the creation rhythms as we admit our frailty and fallenness.

C2: Cross

I can remember sitting around a wood-fuelled stove, listening to the English Church leader Richard Coekin explaining how we need to have a bigger view of the work of

---

17. John Stott, *Favourite Psalms* (London: Monarch Books, 2003), p. 11.

Christ. We must beware of settling for a singular, flattened, proposition. He used a term that has stuck with me and encouraged me to go deeper into the Bible: the gospel diamond. I love that! Coekin described how the gospel is a beautiful diamond that is multifaceted. You can look at it for years, at different angles, and it will always surprise you and bring joy. Perhaps, as a Welsh experiential Calvinist, I would add that the Holy Spirit shines a light on the gospel diamond that brings life and love.

An unintended danger with the modern 'gospel-centred' movement is that it reduces the gospel diamond to a blunt, forensic, statement. Often, any and every problem is met with 'the gospel is the answer'. Yes, but no. Yes, the gospel is always the answer. But no, the word 'gospel' is not. We must look at the riches of God's grace and apply it in a myriad of ways to the many situations in life. The heart is a perpetual forge of idols, but it is not a mass producer of cookie cutter sins.[18] The forge is making bespoke temptations and trials that need made-to-measure solutions. And the gospel diamond does that.

Let's consider one view of the gospel, a facet of the gospel diamond that can release us from the reign of social media, stress and Sabbath-breaking. Back in the first chapter, I shared about the way that the words of Jesus in Mark 6:31 had confounded me in my time of crisis. 'Come with me by yourselves to a quiet place and get some rest.' But I have come to see that those words become sweet when we look at them through the lens of Matthew 11:28, 'Come to me, all who are weary and burdened, and I will give you rest.'

---

18. It was the great reformer Calvin who coined the term 'forge of idols' in *Calvin: Institutes of the Christian Religion, Volume One* (Westminster John Knox Press, Kentucky, p. 108.

It is in coming to Jesus, who has come to us, that we can find true rest. A spiritual and eternal rest that can help us have physical and temporal rest now. Jesus is saying that He Himself is the solution to our stress. He can tell us how to get off the treadmill – with Him. Consider these life-giving words with me.

Jesus knows that we all get wearied and burdened

Isn't that beautiful? Jesus knows. Jesus understands. Because God became man and dwelt among us, He knows us. The Bible says that Jesus can sympathise with us. What wonderful news! When Jesus sees us weary and burdened, He says *'Come'*, *'Come to me'*. This is what we saw with Martha. Jesus knew. But we have more than tea and sympathy. Jesus offers us Ultimate Rest. Jesus is not here offering us a new diary plan. This is not self-help 101, or small tweaks to our coping mechanisms. Rather, Jesus is offering us something more amazing. Himself. All rest in the creation rhythms point us to the spiritual rest found in Jesus.

Jesus came to do what we cannot do, to earn that which we can't earn, and to give what we don't want to give. He gives everything so that we can have it all. The danger with books on digital detoxing and time management is that (even Christian ones) they can simply show us how to manage our sins and stresses, and then be in a place to do them more efficiently and effectively. I want to do something different here. I want us to see Jesus and His life-giving gift of true rest, before we look at anything else.

This is why we need to spend time looking at our weaknesses. As Earley points out so clearly, 'there is more going on than just our body's need for rest. Our souls need rest too. But the rest that our souls need is not simply a nap. It's the rest that comes with realising we don't have anything to prove anymore.'[19]

More facets that free us

As I said earlier, one of the best people I have seen do this is the author Tim Chester. Let's go back to his six heart struggles and look at how he responds to each of them. For each problem, he gives a bespoke gospel solution, and it is wonderful to see.

If you are busy because you are trying to prove yourself and find your worth in work, Chester says that you should remember the liberating rest of God (as above). We need to delve into the wonderful doctrine of justification by faith alone. If you are busy because you are trying to fulfil the expectations of others, Tim points us to the liberating fear of God. When we have a right view of God, other people go back to their right size. We are to live for God, not others.

Perhaps your struggle is the fact that everything is out of control. So, how do we apply the Bible? Look at the liberating rule of God. We need to put the rules of sleep and Sabbath in. See the boundaries that God has laid out, and live within them. We need to believe that God knows best, and that He has everything in control. Maybe, like me, you like to be under pressure. Chester shows how the liberating refuge of God is the answer. We shouldn't try to find satisfaction in the buzz of busyness, but the arms of God.

The pursuit of money and making the most of life were the last two. The antidote to those are the liberating joy of God and liberating hope of God. We need to look to Him

---

19. Earley, p. 147.

and find ourselves in Him. As John Piper reminds us in the book of the same title, God is the gospel. When our view of God and His gospel is too small, we will look elsewhere for joy and hope, and that will ultimately come down to working harder, doing more, and sacrificing for the idols of this world.

Jesus really is the answer. But He is the answer in an array of amazing ways. As we learn to turn from our screens to our Saviour, we will seek the social media serotonin less, and soak in the showers of God's blessings. As we will see in the next chapter, we can even use our smart phones and screens to help us do this.

C3: Consummation

I love the way Chester ends his list with hope. He makes us look beyond our current situation and this life, and reminds us that there is more than meets the eye. The consummation is the fulfilling and enjoyment of all that Jesus has achieved for us. At present, we live in the light of what Jesus has done – it has been inaugurated. But we don't have it all. So, our sins have been forgiven, but we still get tempted and sin. We have been given eternal life, but we still die physically. We call this the 'now and not-yet'. We have the blessings of the gospel now, but there is more to come.

One of the reasons we get so addicted to stress, status, social media, success, soothing media and sinful habits, is because we forget that there is more. There is more to enjoy, more to embrace and more to experience in the here and now, as well as in heaven. Deep down, whilst we cherish our union with Christ, and enjoy moments and seasons of communion with Him, we know there is more.[20] But we forget this and try and fill the void with functional idols.

---

20. I am thankful to Simon Ponsonby and his helpful book *More: How you can*

Living in light of heaven stops us from trying to get every bucket list experience here for fear of FOMO. But it doesn't just stop things; it starts things. When we live in the hope of heaven, we want to make sure that our life echoes into eternity. We want to please the Lord, live on His mission, and hear the words, *'Well done my good and faithful servant.'* We live for more than our seventy years and a good history of Facebook status. We live for God. As we will see, this will make us more compassionate, evangelistic and present in this age (which probably seems counterintuitive at the moment).

Sleep, Sabbath and stopping

This has been a long chapter that has made a deep dive into our identity. But I need to push a little further, a little deeper. You see, behind the creation principles of sleep and Sabbath is the overarching command to stop. To pause. To put down. To push yourself to admit that you are but dust, but God is divine and in control. Ultimately, I am pushing us away from the self and on to the Saviour. But, as Eugene Peterson says, 'the Kingdom of the self is heavily defended territory.'[21] To learn to stop, as we reclaim sleep and Sabbath and apply that to our work and the web, will make for awkward conversations.

The most common question we ask a new acquaintance is 'What do you do?' That is, prove your worth. And the most common question we ask friends is 'What have you been up to?' We then get into a competition of busyness or one-upmanship, that is ultimately an attempt to attain the

have more of the Spirit when you already have everything in Christ (David C. Cook: Colorado Springs, 2009).

21. Eugene Peterson, *The Contemplative Pastor* (Carol Stream, Christianity Today and Word Publishing, 1989) p. 44.

coveted badge of honour that is stretched, stressed, and sleep-deprived.

Can you imagine the scandal of engaging in conversation rather than competition?

But we need to be careful here. There is a dangerous unintended consequence to what I have just written. The temptation to hide our stresses and strains. The error of becoming a duck who seems calm on the surface, but is kicking madly beneath the waters.

Ultimately, I think Curtis Zackery is onto something when he writes, 'Most of us find it challenging to admit that we need a break of any kind – it feels like admitting weakness, and not just being able to power through our fatigue and pains. In our culture, we celebrate busyness because we believe that perpetual motion is an indication of a level of importance.'[22]

The heart is a complex thing. It is like the Polymorph in Red Dwarf – a shape-shifting creature that steals emotions. Our hearts keep shifting from one error to another, trying to grab our emotions of joy and peace.

Let's pause here.

I wonder, why are you reading this book?

Be honest.

Could it be that you want someone to come alongside you and say, 'Stop', 'Slow down', '*Selah*'. Sometimes, we need someone to give us permission to get off the rollercoaster of life.

As I sit here and write these words in a coffee shop, I am praying for you … and I am praying Psalm 46 for you. God really can be your refuge in the stress and your strength in

---

22. Zackery, p. 21.

the strain. He is ever-present, ready to be your help. It may seem like the earth is giving way and the mountains are crashing down around you. But, there is a river that can make you glad, waters that can refresh rather than roar. Jesus is the water of life. We need to be still … and know that our refuge and strength is God Almighty.

I can remember the day I was driving down the dual carriageway with pains in my chest and a numb arm. Tears started rolling down my cheeks as I thought of how much work I had to do and how little of my family I had seen. I was desperate to serve others … but I was also deceived by my own desire to make much of myself. I needed to be able to stop. I needed to slow down. Thankfully, I plucked up the courage to turn around and see my GP. That night, as I spoke to me wife, her grace and gentleness reflected that of the Lord's, and she spoke the words I needed to hear. Stop.

So, take a deep breath and listen up, let me be the one who says to you 'stop' as an under-shepherd to the One who says 'be still.'

This is the Interruption we all need.

Selah

1. Has anything stood out to you in this chapter? What was it? Why?

2. Do you think about frailty as a good thing?

3. How do you feel about having a weekly Sabbath?

4. Which of Chester's six heart motivations do you identify with?

5. Do you need to stop?

Prayer

Creator God, Thank You for making us in Your image, with the capacity to know and enjoy You. Forgive me for thinking that I am created equal to You, able to be everywhere, know everyone and do everything. Help me to remember that I am dust, and that I can Sabbath, sleep and Selah in light of Your goodness and grace. In the name of Jesus, Amen.

Transition

Now we are coming to the heart of this book. The reason I wrote it. Having proven that there are intentional interruptions in our lives that distract us, but that God has Intentional Interruptions that are divine, I want to help you to switch from the distraction to the divine. To change the intentions of your life. Not from the intentions of others to yours, but from others' to God's. In essence, I want to help you change the default setting of your life.

How do we know the way? How do we know what to do and what not to do? With technologies and society and life-change at a constant pace, how can we seriously know how to respond to everything?

Come with me back up to the Black Mountains. On that lovely weekend camping trip. When we were walking we had no phones, watches or maps, nothing. But our group leader was amazing. He knew every bump, every rock collection, every flower, every part of the local history.

There was nothing that he didn't know about our trip. I loved spending time with him, learning about and loving all that was surrounding us.

But guess what … He had never been on that mountain. In fact, he had never been to the area before! I and the men from my church all lived within five miles of the mountain, he lived 500 miles away, and had spent a large chunk of the last ten years in China. But yet, he knew everything. How? Because he had a map and he was a map reader.

The Bible is our map that is timeless, and can guide us through any developments in life and society. And the wonderful news is, we not only have the map, but the map reader, the Holy Spirit. And so, we can still rely on the Bible today to help us navigate the new technologies and media. The Bible can show us two things. Firstly, it can show us what to guard against. It gives us principles that work across cultures and centuries, and through the Spirit it can go beneath the presenting issue, to the heart of the matter. Secondly, we can look at what it tells us to gaze upon. The Bible tells us the kinds of things we should put our minds to. And, using these biblical insights, we can look at what others have written and taught about these new struggles, and wisely discern them and apply them with divine help.

In my early days of using computers and smart phones, I didn't realise that they had default settings that I could change. I thought that how they came was how they had to be used. But, with each passing generation of my iPhone and upgrade of the latest apps, I have started to become a bit more tech savvy. I now go into the settings and change things. Notifications? Off. Open automatically when you turn on your device? Off. Sit on your home screen, enticing you to check it? Off! I have learnt to change who is the master and who is the slave. My iPhone is no longer my master, barking commands at what I must read, listen to, do or buy. Rather, through some little changes in the default settings and the liturgies of my life, I have made my iPhone a slave to my desires. But I have had to make sure that those are Spirit-empowered, gospel-saturated, Bible-informed, desires.

This means that changing lower-case interruptions for upper-case Interruptions is not simply about your heart or your handset. Rather, it is about both. To live truly the life Christ wants for us, we need to change the default setting in both our heart and our handset, our souls and our screens, our worldview and the World Wide Web.

5

Just Say No
Principles and practicalities to enable you to say 'yes' to Jesus

The seven habits of highly _____ people.

What would you fill that blank with? Maybe you know it's a book title and add the word 'effective'.[1] But that is not what I am aiming for. You know that already. Having re-orientated ourselves and thought about our true identity, we can now look at ways of taking back control of our smart phones and social media. But this is for far more than efficiency, effectiveness or even excellence. This is for glory. Not ours, but God's.

In this chapter, we are going to drill down and consider seven 'keystone' habits that will change the default settings of our handsets and hearts. These are the fruit of the last chapter and will ultimately create friction for our lower-case interruptions and remove the barriers to our upper-case Interruptions. In doing this, I hope that we won't just have more time, but that we will get rid of our restless, distracted hurry, and have more time for God and His glory.

---

1. Stephen Covey, *The Seven Habits of Highly Effective Leaders* (London: Simon & Schuster UK, 2020).

One: Set your sight on the Saviour

We must work on our heart first. Whatever habits we create, they need to be an overflow of the affections. Ultimately, our heart is the default and direction-setting fountain of our life. Our heart is what leads and directs us. I have found Jefferson Bethke helpful in his book *To Hell with the Hustle* on the depth of habits:

> Here's the thing about habits: they are less about doing something and more about loving something. We sleep with our phones right by our bed, sometimes even under our pillows, not just because we actively make a choice every morning to look at the news in the world or what our friends are doing. We do it because we love what the phone gives us. There is an ancient call in us that taps the spigot of our desires until the ritual becomes worshipful and mundane.[2]

It all starts with the heart.

I am trying to create the opposite of a spiral to despair. That is, when we let the pings control us, we end up missing the upper-case Interruptions, the divine encounters, and so we rely more on the security, status and satisfaction that social media and work give us. We end up needing those interruptions. They become addictive.

Chapter 4 gave us a road map on this. Acknowledge your frailty and fallenness, and in the acts of slowing, sleep and Sabbath look forward to the gospel. We need to look closely at those rhythms and make the links. Sleep reminds us of death, but it also reminds us that through Jesus, death can be redefined as sleep. Jesus has beaten death, the tomb is empty. Hallelujah! And what about the Sabbath? There is

---

2. Bethke, p. 18.

an ultimate Sabbath rest, the Lord Jesus. The church moved the Sabbath principle from the end of the week (Saturday) to the first day of the week (Sunday) for two reasons. Firstly, it shows that the resurrection is the start of our new life. It changes everything. Secondly, it radically reveals that we rest before we work. We get a day off in grace, before we can even try to earn it.

Surround the sleep and Sabbath rhythms with *Selahs* that focus on the goodness and gospel of Jesus. Read the Bible, look to Jesus, ensure that you are preaching the gospel to yourself. This is the first and fundamental step to learning to say 'no' to the interruptions of the world, and open yourself up to the divine Interruptions that the Lord has in store for you. Those are the big take-aways that the Bible gives us as the map to guide us through the choppy waters of contemporary ways.

So, as Paul tells us, we need to set our hearts on things above, be transformed by the renewing of our minds, think upon the good, and grasp how wide and long and high and deep is the love of Christ.[3] If we start with Jesus, then curate our interruptions, create new habits and liturgies, and give time to divine Interruptions, we will see more of Jesus. It is an ever-increasing sense of God's presence.

So, work on your heart.

I love the way an old hymn puts it:

> Give me a sight, O Saviour,
> Of Thy wondrous love to me,
> Of the love that bro't Thee down to earth,
> To die on Calvary.

---

3. Colossians 3:3; Romans 12:2; Philippians 4:8; Ephesians 3:18.

Oh, make me understand it,
Help me to take it in,
What it meant to Thee, the Holy One,
To bear away my sin.[4]

We would do well to say with the Greeks in John 12:21, 'Sir, we would like to see Jesus.'

Two: Switch off your notifications and create a social media-free screen

This is probably the simplest step. An easy win. But the benefits are tremendous. Notifications are one of the most potent parts of any strategy to interrupt us. You could be watching your first-born child receive a school prize and still be caught by the glare of a notification in the corner of your eye. Honestly, the amount of times I have seen people look down to a blinking screen as I talk to them is demoralising. It screams out that the screen is more important than me.

Make Time is excellent on this. In the midst of their eighty tactics to 'focus on what matters every day', right at the heart of the book is the chapter titled 'Be the boss of your own phone.'[5] The authors share how they both moved to distraction-free phones in 2012 as they realised that their mobiles were like the Ring to Bilbo Baggins and Kryptonite to Superman. The alerts and ads that came up on their screen were both demanding and damaging.

The answer is simple. Delete social media apps, games, news apps, streaming services, email, and the web browser. Get rid of anything that is what they call an 'infinity pool' – a place of never-ending interest. In effect, you are creating

---

4. K. A. M. Kelly (1869-1942).
5. Knapp, the following quotations come from pp. 91-103.

a 'dumb phone'. It's like having a Nokia brick again (if you are old enough to remember that awesome phone), but without the snake game. But, it isn't quite that drastic. They still keep maps, music apps, Uber, calendars, weather apps, and other tools that 'don't make you twitchy'.

And with that cull of apps, you can turn off all the notifications too. I laughed out loud when I read their mission: 'By turning off your notifications, you'll teach your phone some manners. You'll transform it from a nonstop blabbering loudmouth into a polite bearer of important news – the kind of friend you'd actually want in your life.' Oh, to have a well-behaved phone!

However, as we will see in the seventh keystone, we are not going to clear our devices completely. We are not rejecting modern technology, but redeeming it.

We are simply creating friction to get to our distractions. Making it harder.

Three: Sleep without a screen and start the day with Scripture

In his excellent book *The Tech-Wise Family*, Andy Crouch makes a startling claim: 'Nothing about our lives at home has been so thoroughly disrupted by technology as sleep.'[6] We have already seen that God wants us to sleep. But the phone stops that. I wonder, why do you take your phone to bed? Is it simply as an alarm? Or are you scared someone might phone and you'll miss it? I find I create a myriad of reasons to keep my phone next to my head in bed.

But Crouch is surely right when he says, 'the devices we carry to bed to make us feel connected and safe actually

---

6. Andy Crouch, *The Tech-Wise Family*, (Michigan: Baker Books, 2017), p. 114.

prevent us from trusting in the One who knows our needs and who alone can protect us through the dangers and sorrows of every night.[7] We simply must leave our devices outside the bedroom. We need to draw near to the Divine, not our devices. We need God, not gossiping newsfeeds.

There will be two instant benefits to a bed without screens. Firstly, you will sleep better physically as it helps to create an environment of absolute darkness. It lets your mind slow down, and your heart settle. Secondly, when you wake up you will be more refreshed and ready to read your Bible. You see, this isn't about merely having more sleep, but hearing more Scripture.

Our days are set by the things we read first. Have you ever noticed that? A sad news day can send us grumpily to work. A harsh email sent at night and read first thing, can make us growl at the kids. And a ringing reminder of the long list of jobs we need to get through, can put us into stress mode before we have had time to pray. That is why it is vital that we read the Bible before anything else.

Whilst in the second habit we were adding friction to our interruptions, here we are getting rid of friction for God's Word.

These rhythms are so important. You can think of them as habits. Earlier in the book we looked at *The Common Rule* by Earley and considered how keystone habits can have a negative effect on our life, but they can have a positive one too. Actually, the habits we change can be 'the first domino in the line; by changing one habit, we simultaneously change ten other habits.'[8] Embrace the domino effect. Stop looking at your phone first thing in the morning. It is an

---

7. Ibid., p. 118.
8. Earley, p. 36.

electronic Tardis that opens us up to a world of highs and lows, truths and lies, hopes and fears.

According to Earley, there are three wrong morning habits that we can slip into. Firstly, work emails; secondly, news updates; thirdly, social media. All three will set your heart and mind in an unhelpful direction. Work emails can cause stress, the news can create anger, and social media can do any number of things. Yet, in the first five minutes of your day, a simple and significant change of habit can give you a phenomenal spiritual formation that can change your day, and your life. The dominoes will fall to reveal a beautiful image of Christ formed in your heart. Simply swap the smart phone for the quiet time. How old school is that?!

Listen to Earley explain it simply:

> My smartphone exacerbates my tendency toward self-centred or legalistic morning prayers. Why? Because, of course, my phone is the portal through which the chaos of the world reaches my half-asleep heart through the pesky things we call 'notifications.' This inevitably begins my day with all that I need to do and all that I've failed to do. Our phones – and their programmers – are happy to set our habits for us. They would love to speak the first words of the day, and they usually do.[9]

Don't let the 'interruption' of your phone as you open your eyes rule your heart. Throw it out of your bedroom. Look to the Bible and talk to God before you do anything else. Let God set your agenda, settle your heart, and set you up for the day.

---

9. Ibid., p. 35.

Do you want me to buy a dumb phone?

Not really, no.

I love my iPhone. I'll be honest: it's linked to my Mac and lots of my work, hobbies, fun and family photos. But, I also know that I am like Bilbo Baggins with the Ring, and there is a sense in which I need to keep a close eye on who is the boss: me or the phone. My devices are great tools, but they can easily become gnarly task masters.

So, I may need to have a dumb phone one day. You may need to get rid of your smart phone now – but only you can make that decision. But the phone itself is not evil. In fact, the phone can be used for good. Even for your spiritual formation! We can redeem it.

A good friend of mine who read an early draft of this book, and has culled social media, did gently push back that perhaps more people should give up their smart phones. I found that helpful. Perhaps in trying to take a moderate position I am leaning too far towards 'redeeming' the tech. Maybe life would be better if we simply got out of the social media frenzy and had phones for old-school communication. Maybe that is a path for you.

Four: Start having a screen-free Sabbath

I think this is the hardest, but the most rewarding, of the habits. Both Dr Chatterjee in his secular book and Justin Earley in his Christian book, encourage a complete day of rest from screens. This is genuinely the most radical, and it gives an amazing reward. A day without screens, social media and streaming services is a sweet sabbath. It not only changes your day, but it transforms your week.

The first day I tried a fast from tech was a LONG day! I spent the whole time wondering what I was missing out on.

FOMO was fierce. But then I started to notice some things. My concentration got longer, my attention got deeper, and enjoyment of others got better. It was as if a load was lifted from my shoulders, and I could be present in the moment.

The great thing about taking a weekly break from the blinking screens is that it disrupts the addiction. You realise that the world doesn't stop and that the sky doesn't fall. Everything is okay. People can wait for email replies, influencers don't lose their income become you didn't like their Instagram, and your thumb didn't fall off because you didn't scroll through Twitter. Actually, you just end up enjoying more and being free to hold your phone less dearly and nearly the next day. It breaks the cycle.

I love how Bethke brings this all to a conclusion by writing: 'While some like to say they keep the Sabbath, we know the Sabbath keeps us.'[10]

Five: Savour silence and solitude (be bored!)

Once you have started to enjoy God and been able to ignore your phone, you can start to practise some ancient spiritual disciplines. I was first introduced to these practices through the writing of Richard Foster, and in particular *Celebration of Discipline*. Whist there is much in the book I would question, there is a lot of wisdom in his chapter on Solitude. This is something that very few of us practise any more. In fact, even when we are physically alone, the screens we carry ensure we are never truly on our own.

Why have we created a world where it is hard to experience solitude? Foster is surely right when he says that 'the fear of being left alone petrifies people.'[11] When

10. Bethke, p. 147.
11. Richard Foster, *The Celebration of Discipline* (London: Hodder and Stoughton, 2000), p. 121.

he wrote the book back in the 1970s, he saw that 'our fear of being alone drives us to noise and crowds.' But forty years on, I think we are now driven to WhatsApp groups, Facebook pages and online forums. Now, we can run from solitude in a computer rather than a crowd.

But we need to embrace solitude, silence and *selah*. We need to welcome them. And the only way to do that is to create space in our day. The habits above do just that. By starting your day with Scripture, turning off all notifications, and learning to say 'no', we can say 'yes' to free time and silence. And yes, even boredom.

I find the hardest battle is trying not to pick up my phone when I have a free moment.

But, once we create that outer silence, we can start to work on an inner silence. And that is cyclical. Once we gain inner silence, we are happier with outer silence (we will explore this more in Chapter 9 and the conscience). Silence and solitude are much-needed spiritual disciplines.

Bethke explains why:

When we first think of silence and solitude, we may not care much about it, or we may even think it sounds religiously sexy and hipster, cool, and trendy. Until we try it. And then we are shocked and maybe terrified by it. Because in silence we feel exposed and naked, and weirdly we become noisy. Not outwardly but inside our heads. So we quickly dismiss it. Nah, I'm good. But here's the unsexy and unpolished truth: our aversion to that nakedness and the awkwardness and ugliness we feel are actually why we need to do it.[12]

---

12. Bethke, p. 121.

Later, Bethke expresses exactly what I want to declare: 'My new life mantra is: be boring.'[13] Why do we feel like this? 'Because what our culture defines as boring (or mediocre or wasteful squandering of talent), the Scriptures and the way of Jesus define as quiet, beautiful, faithful.'[14]

So, seek silence. Be bored.

Six: Speak to people without a screen

I don't want this book to be an individualistic pursuit of esoteric spirituality. We need community – we were created for it. So far you could be forgiven for thinking I am proposing a sort of modern monastic method of living. But I am not. Although maybe I am! You see, monks lived in community and served the community. They didn't all take vows of silence and spend their days ornately crafting calligraphed copies of the canon. No, they worshipped, walked, and worked together. In community. They opened schools, hospitals, and food pantries. They lived their life free from as many worldly distractions as possible so that they could serve the Lord.

In a sense I am edging towards that kind of monastic mission.

And so, when we lift our gaze from social media we should become more socially-minded. We should remember how to relate to people. For, let's be honest, our digital dialogues leave a lot to be desired. We learn to demand, shout, over-react, cut off, cancel and ignore others online. Moreover, we have enjoyed the fact that with the World Wide Web we can always find people who are easier to get on with, less demanding or challenging, and more self-serving.

---

13. Ibid., p. 123.
14. Ibid., p. 123.

The Covid pandemic showed us the danger of losing physical contact and fellowship. Yes, it introduced us to the advantages of Zoom and live streaming. But it also demonstrated that, in the end, digital is not the best. It has its place, but we need to see people in person. That is healthier.

In his excellent book *Analog Church*, Jay Kim shows how the digital age has created a problem in the midst of its potential:

> The digital age's technological advancements boast three major contributions to the improvement of human experience, which in turn have become its undeniable values: 1. Speed. We have access to what we want when we want, as quickly as our fingers can type and scroll. 2. Choices. We have access to an endless array of options when it comes to just about anything. 3. Individualism. Everything, from online profiles to gadgets, is endlessly customizable, allowing us to emphasize our preferences and personalities.[15]

He goes on to expose the dangers:

> Social media is fuelled by voyeurism—that broken inclination within each of us to peek behind the curtain of other people's lives. Rather than connecting us, the voyeuristic nature of social media actually detaches and distances us from one another, as we find ourselves running aimlessly on the treadmill of comparison and contempt. We feel like we can see one another's lives, but none of us ever feel truly seen.[16]

---

15. Jay Kim, *Analog Church* (Grand Rapids, IVP, 2020), p. 19.
16. Ibid., p. 23.

Wow, do I use social media as a form of voyeurism? Am I curating and presenting a version of myself that means people don't really know the true me?

Thankfully, Christians and the church can lead the way in being a people focused:

> In the digital age, one of the most upside down things the church can offer is the invitation to be analog, to come out of hiding from behind our digital walls, to bridge our technological divides, and to be human with one another in the truest sense—gathering together to be changed and transformed in real time, in real space, in real ways.[17]

We should make time to see people in person. It is better and more honest. Oh, and safer. Bethke gives us a warning about our online communications:

> Trying to understand each other should be normal, but sadly it is becoming almost a superpower in our culture to have the ability to really lean into someone's point of view and gain true understanding and nuance first before we respond. Instead, Internet culture rewards straw-man fallacies times a million, but as followers of Jesus, we really have to check ourselves in how we communicate with others, because frankly we are killing ourselves over it.[18]

Seven: Select what serves you best

One of the favourite series of books my wife and I have read with our three boys are the *You Choose* series. They are big, colourful books that give you oodles of odd things to choose from: where would you like to live (a castle or a cave); what hat would you like to wear (a bowler hat or

---

17. Ibid., p. 16.
18. Bethke, p. 173.

baseball cap); and so on. The joy of the book is having the choice and then sharing why. Obviously, we all want to live in a cave with a bowler hat because castles and baseball caps are a dime a dozen in Wales.

I love the idea of curating media and communication. Choosing what you want. So many thinkers suggest this. You see, we don't need to take a hammer to crack a walnut. It is needless to get rid of everything. They key is, choose the best. Make decisions. You choose. Go for things that are tools and not task masters. Enjoy apps that serve you.

As a family we love WhatsApp; it helps us stay in contact. As a Christian, I love my prayer and reading apps. They help me work efficiently and fill my mind with good things. There is a way to choose the best and be connected to others in a good and healthy way.

Habits create a rhythm

We are trying to create new habits because, taken together, they will form a new rhythm. Bethke asks the question if we know which rhythm we are dancing to – the world, or the Lord? I love that image. It is hard to dance out of rhythm, but we must do that with the world. Don't let others set your agenda. Let the Lord. And that is the good news. It is easier to get out of step with the world's line-dance when you join the Lord's *twmpath*[19] (I am assuming that Welsh folk-dancing represents God's goodness). When we follow the rhythm of the Lord, we will find a much better way of life.

My friend Peter Mead changes the image beautifully and says that we are like a bride with the bridegroom on their first dance. It is filled with love and the bride will do well to

---

19. *Twmpath* is a Welsh word for our version of a Ceilidh or Barn Dance.

follow the bridegroom's lead. When she does, she is swept up in his arms and swirls freely and lovingly around the room.

We need to learn to keep in step with the Spirit in our use and non-use of screens. And then, we will learn to dance with, and delight in, our wonderful Saviour.

Selah

1. Has anything stood out to you here?

2. Is there a habit you could start to implement today?

3. Was that habit the first one? If not, why not? How could you start to set your sight on the Saviour?

Prayer

Give me a sight, O Saviour,
Of Thy wondrous love to me,
Of the love that bro't Thee down to earth,
To die on Calvary.

Oh, make me understand it,
Help me to take it in,
What it meant to Thee, the Holy One,
To bear away my sin.
Amen.[20]

---

20. K. A. M. Kelly (1869-1942).

Part 2

6

Creation

It took a few seconds for my brain to understand what was happening. It was pitch black, apart from the glow of my iPhone, which was beeping with regular alarm. What was going on? What day was it? Who was calling me in the middle of the night? But then it all came flooding back. I had set the alarm on my phone ... for 4:30 am! As the realisation dawned, I remembered I was going to take my two oldest boys up a local mountain to see the sunrise. I tiptoed across the landing, trying not to wake my wife or youngest child, and gently woke the boys from their deep sleep. They moaned, but then started to move as they remembered the plan. Hiking up a mountain in the dark, with only some little torches to guide us, and then a victor's breakfast on top of the Sugar Loaf as we watched the day begin.

It took just under two hours to get to the peak, and it was only the promise of hot chocolate and croissant that kept us going. To be honest, the sense of adventure and fun only lasted about ten minutes. The reality of walking in the cold darkness wasn't as great as we had envisioned. The last section of the walk is a pretty steep climb, and the conversation was definitely getting more and more frustrating ... for all of us. But then, with perfect timing, we edged on to the top of the mountain, took a deep breath, and looked over to our right. From behind The Skirrid (The Holy Mountain of Abergavenny) we saw the sun rise. We *felt* it too. Our eyes were filled with the glow of orange, and our bones were warmed by the rays of light. The three of us sat silently as the sky took over the conversation. The speech that poured forth was so fascinating that none of us wanted to interrupt.

Those three minutes were some of the most powerful I have ever experienced.

Are we there yet?

As a parent, one of the debates I have every year is whether to put a DVD player (or iPad) in the back of the car. They can certainly make a long journey much easier when there are children whining 'are we there yet?'! But they also have an unintended consequence of children ignoring the parent who says, 'look', 'consider' … 'see'. Aren't the children missing something if we let them stare at a screen – left to their own devices? Isn't the reality of creation more amazing than the banality of animation? But, could it be that as adults we have done the same? That is, we have metaphorical DVD players of worries playing in our minds, or iPads of worldly pleasures in our daydreams, in this journey we call life. Do we live life at a pace that does not allow us to see? Restlessly asking 'are we there yet?' and missing the life and light that is right in front of our eyes now.

Have you ever driven home from work and not looked at the local hill or a sunset with awe – but rather just wanted to get home and sleep? Or have you been so stressed that you missed an entire spring of blossom at the bottom of the garden? Perhaps you know what it is not to have had time to stop to watch the sunset. But then, does it matter? Is noticing these things a good and Christian use of time? Should we waste our time staring at some flowers? Is it a wise use of energy to wait up and lie under the stars? Should we get our binoculars and watch the birds? Especially when we consider the needs of our friends, family, neighbours, church and society. Is looking at creation a Christian pursuit?

I'll be honest: I didn't use to think so. I took passages like Colossians 4 seriously, where Paul says we need to make the most of every opportunity, buying up time for the sake of the gospel. But then, I started to notice something Jesus did. I saw those times when He used to interrupt people and teach them things, pointing out parts of creation. How He got the disciples to turn off the DVD player and look out the car window. He got them to stop and consider the … Well, you know where I'm going with this. But do you *really* know it?

Look and see

In Matthew chapter 6, Jesus gives a powerful command to His hearers in the Sermon on the Mount: 'Look' (verse 26). Jesus wanted His disciples to look. That word doesn't mean glance or remember. Rather, the word means: Look closely, directly, be attentive. This word is used throughout the New Testament in powerful ways. For example, in Mark 10:21, we see Jesus looked and loved the young man. He really saw him. In Luke 22:61, we see Jesus looking at Peter – and what a stare that was! These were life-changing looks.

Jesus then adds a second word in verse 28: 'See'. That means to gaze, contemplate. The passage is clear: Jesus wants us to look at creation and contemplate. Many Christians over the centuries have done this – looked at creation, or just been in nature – and it has had profound effects on them. Let me share three examples.

Nearly 300 years ago in America, the brilliant theologian Jonathan Edwards wrote in his diary: 'Sometimes on fair days I find myself more particularly disposed to regard the glories of the world than to betake myself to the study of serious religion.'[1] This is no small thing for him to say. Edwards is considered the greatest American theologian, and he had a phenomenal ability to study and write. But, yet, creation was something that could captivate him, and give him space to be captivated by God. And so, he would leave his study and go out to see.

Edwards describes one of these occasions:

Once as I rode out into the woods for my health in 1737, having alighted from my horse in a retired place, as my manner commonly has been, to walk for divine contemplation and prayer, I had a view, that for me was extraordinary, of the glory of the Son of God, as Mediator between God and man, and his wonderful, great, full, pure and sweet grace and love and meek, gentle condescension. This grace that appeared so calm and sweet appeared also great above the heavens. The person of Christ appeared ineffably excellent, with an excellency great enough to swallow up all thought and conception—which continued, as near as I can judge, about an hour; which kept me the greater part of the time in a flood of tears, and weeping aloud. I felt an ardency of soul to be what I know not otherwise how to express, emptied and annihilated; to lie in the dust; and to be full of Christ alone; to love him;

---

1. Jonathan Edwards, *The Works of Jonathan Edwards, Vol. 1* (Edinburgh: The Banner of Truth, 1998), p. xlvii.

to serve and follow him; and to be perfectly sanctified and made pure, with a divine and heavenly purity. I have several other times had views very much of the same nature, and which have had the same effects.[2]

Closer to our time, and in the UK, the Anglican minister John Stott was famous for his bird watching. When he would travel the world to share the gospel and teach the Bible, he would often take time out to enjoy ornithology. This was something he was encouraged to do by those who cared for him and knew what would be good for his long-term mental health and ministry. I loved the recording of him preaching at Keswick one year on 1 Corinthians, and sharing how he was watching a little bird fly at the back of the convention tent. He even went on to write a book about birds and how they can be our teachers.

One contemporary writer who demonstrates a thoughtfulness about creation is Tim Chester, in his book on the Trinity. Even in that context, he is able to give a wonderful exploration of such things as water and the leaf. Listen to what he writes:

You have no reason to be bored – not in God's world. We live in a world with an excess of beauty, a redundancy of beauty. Think about a leaf. Every leaf is unique. God could have saved a lot of bother. He could have made a world in which leaves were like plastic cups, punched out to the same design. But every leaf is handmade. And every leaf is a thing of exquisite beauty.[3]

2. Ibid.

3. Tim Chester, *Enjoying God*, (London:The Good Book Company, 2019), p. 45.

Just looking at a leaf can teach us about God. His character. Who He is and what He is like. These are the kind of things that Jesus wanted us to notice. We are meant to stop and stare, pause and ponder, and carve out time to consider creation. I sat down and read through the Gospel of Matthew one morning, and noted how Jesus kept referring to creation:

- Matthew 4: see the sun come into the darkness
- Sermon on the Mount: see how the sun rises on the righteous and unrighteous (and rain)
- Sermon on the Mount: see the good tree and bad tree
- Sermon on the Mount: consider the rock as a foundation for a house
- Matthew 9: imagine those sheep without a shepherd; look at how the harvest is plentiful
- Matthew 10: see those sparrows being sold
- Matthew 12: consider a bruised reed
- Matthew 13: in The Parable of the Sower, look at the fields and farmer

I could go on. It seems that Jesus intended for us to look at creation and be Interrupted. To see.

Here is a question for you: Are these random illustrations? Things that 'just so happen' to teach us something? Or were they designed in creation for this purpose? To put it another way, is creation merely illustrational, or masterfully intentional? Did God think of these illustrations after He created the world? Or did He create them that way for the illustrations? You may have thought about this in other ways before, like whether marriage is primarily about marriage or the gospel?

Okay, let me explain what I mean. Let's start with what we can agree on.

I think there are three things we can agree on. One, God has made some things specifically always to communicate a specific message. The rainbow is a classic example of that. God created the rainbow to teach us that He would never flood the world again. Two, God uses some things at specific times to communicate. For example, the star shining in the sky for the birth of Jesus. And thirdly, God has created all things generally to reveal His glory. The Cappadocian church father, Basil of Caesarea, wrote that 'each of the things that have been made fulfils its own particular purpose in creation … Not a single one of these things is without worth, not a single thing has been created without a reason.'

Many of us have known this from childhood. We sang about it in school assemblies …

All things bright and beautiful,
All creatures great and small,
All things wise and wonderful:
The Lord God made them all.

Each little flow'r that opens,
Each little bird that sings,
He made their glowing colors,
He made their tiny wings.

The purple-headed mountains,
The river running by,
The sunset and the morning
That brightens up the sky.[4]

---

4. Cecil Frances Alexander (1848).

What inspired this song? Well, if you ask people where I live, it was probably the Sugar Loaf mountain that my boys and I climbed, or the Blorenge on the other side of town. Or maybe not. But it was certainly Psalm 104:24:

> How many are your works, LORD!
> In wisdom you made them all;
> the earth is full of your creatures.

God made everything in wisdom. Everything. I think that God speaks in specific ways through specific creations today, and that sometimes He wants to say more through things than just a general revelation of glory. Now, before you think I am going down a very dangerous rabbit hole, let me tell you what I am not saying. I am not saying that creation is enough to communicate salvation (Romans is clear on that), and I am not saying that creation can give additional messages from God (Revelation is clear on that one). So, don't panic.

But I am saying that we can develop our understanding of God's creation, and learn to think about God with it. How? Through reading the Bible. In a sense, it goes two ways: the Bible helps us read creation, and creation helps us read the Bible. However, we must make sure that the Bible is in the driving seat – the interpretive authority.

Learn to read

For this to develop you need two things: a Bible and some time. Perhaps you may want to pick up a Bible and walk outside for this part of the book. Or, if it's raining, look out the window. Turn to Matthew 6 with me. Let's see what Jesus teaches us by getting us to look. Firstly, He opens our eyes to the birds (v. 26). Jesus and the Bible tell us to look at our feathered friends. Generally, to see that God is glorious. Specifically, to realise that God is our provider. And, moreover, to grasp afresh that God is our heavenly Father.

Do you remember how birds show God's provision in the Bible? Noah's ark? The sacrificial system for the tabernacle and Temple? Come to the New Testament, what is the greatest gift according to Jesus? The one that we can ask for and receive? The Holy Spirit, who is symbolised as a dove! And so, when we look at the birds, we should remember that God is glorious, and is our generous heavenly Father. That is what Jesus is saying in the Sermon on the Mount. Have you stopped to look at our feathered friends and thought about that?

A friend and I were filming a documentary in the wilds of mid-Wales. To be honest, we were taking drone shots of graves (yes, that is something that Welsh church historians do for 'fun'). But then I glanced a red kite in the distance, soaring up and around us. We gently sent the drone after it, and followed it landing on a distant tree. As we watched through the camera, we gasped as the red kite took flight and flew past the lens and showed us an effortless beauty and majesty that even the greatest practised Red Devils parachute team couldn't hope to pull off.

Looking back over the footage on a higher definition screen I was reminded of God's glorious design. Of how He made everything in this world, all the birds of the air, and our eyes to see them. But, more than that, He cared for that red kite … provided for him. He could only soar because we have a Sovereign God. So, as Jesus taught us, how much more will our Heavenly Father, who gave us His only Son, give us all things? He cares. He loves. See?

But Jesus doesn't stop there; He takes our gaze and moves us downwards to look at the flowers (v. 28). Birds are creations that are complex and live for years. Flowers are simple and short-lived. Here today, gone tomorrow. Even the most stunning flowers will wither. But is there a specific meaning to plants, flowers and grass? Yes. Lots. What is it here? Well, Jesus tells us plainly: God is generous in clothing them … even though they are thrown away. This is where we come to the meaning of plants. Think about grass …

> The life of mortals is like grass,
> they flourish like a flower of the field;
> the wind blows over it and it is gone,
> and its place remembers it no more.
> (Ps. 103:15-16)

> For,
> 'All people are like grass,
> and all their glory is like the flowers of the field;
> the grass withers and the flowers fall,
> but the word of the Lord endures forever.'
> (1 Pet.1:24-25, quoting Isaiah)

Plants teach us an awful lot. In fact, they should give us an existential crisis! Or, for the Christian, give us a sense of trust and peace that is phenomenal. Jesus picks up those themes. These 'throw away' plants are more splendid than Solomon! But they are not children of God. So, how much more will God care for you – your Heavenly Father? You see we are meant to watch the blossom and go 'Wow – that was over fast … life is over fast … am I ready? But – look how beautiful it is … if God takes so much time on that –

how much more me? He gave His Son, Jesus, to die for me. I can live forever!'

Do you see how we can learn to read creation from the Bible, and the Bible from creation? We are meant to see these things.

I'll be honest: this is just the tip of the iceberg. There is loads more to learn and love. If you want to read more about this then I can recommend two books to you. The first is a big one, that is quite technical, and at points, head scratching. It is called *Through New Eyes: Developing a Biblical View of the World* by James B. Jordan. This is a fascinating look at the symbolic meanings of the sun, moon, stars, rocks, gold, gems, trees, thorns, and many, many more parts of creation. But, if that 330-page tome is too much for you, then there is always the wonderful and wise Andrew Wilson. He has written a short and devotionally sweet book called *God of All Things: Rediscovering the Sacred in an Everyday World*. In 200 pages he opens us up to understanding dust, earthquakes, pigs, honey, mountains, donkeys, and more.

Challenge

In our busy lives, many of us don't have time to see the seasonal change, the beauty of creation, the joy of horticulture or ornithology. But, having slowed down … I wonder … could we re-introduce these things into our New Normal? Could we let God Interrupt us with His amazing creation, and just like my boys on the summit at sunrise, take a moment to quieten our hearts and hear His voice? I wonder, could we, like Jonathan Edwards, walk into the forest and find ourselves in 'flood of tears, and weeping aloud'?

I wonder … Does Jesus want you to stop and savour creation? More than that, to see Him?

Yes!

Yes He does.

So, set your alarm clock, get your thermos of hot chocolate ready, and wake up to see the Son rise.

Selah

1. Have you ever looked at a view of creation that has caused your heart to sing? Where and when was it?

2. When was the last time that happened?

3. Is there somewhere local that you could go and enjoy creation?

Prayer

Creator God,
I lift up my eyes to the mountains—
where does my help come from?
My help comes from the LORD,
the Maker of heaven and earth.[5]

Help me to lift my eyes to the creation
and to You every day.
Amen.

---

5. Psalm 121:1.

7

Compassion

We'd been standing in a huge cattle shed for about an hour and my feet and voice were growing tired. Finally, the musicians put their instruments down and the preacher walked up to the microphone. Yep, I was at a classic shed-based youth conference at the end of the last millennium. I was a new Christian, desperate to serve the Lord in any way I could, and that night the preacher delivered a talk that shocked me in two ways. Firstly, he swore! That was pretty new to a Welshman who was used to a strict diet of three services on a Sunday each requiring adherence to a strict three-piece suit dress code.

But secondly, and most importantly, it was the subject matter of his choice language that unsettled me the most. I can't remember the passage or the points, but I can still hear the clicking of his fingers as he described the plight of the poor and the regularity with which children were dying in poverty. It was the ultimate Bono moment.[1] It should have been heartbreaking. But, if I'm being completely honest, my heart wasn't in it. I just wanted to go to the scheduled late-night gig. And that's when it happened ... he swore.

---

1. Bono is the lead singer of U2, and campaigned to end poverty using a 'click of the fingers' advert.

And in doing so called me out; along with everyone present who had as little emotional investment as I did. He shouted at us and said that we 'didn't give a _____' (a word suitable for a cow shed but not a Christian book). He had my attention – and, as a religious boy studying a degree in theology, I was aghast.

Then he delivered the killer line: 'You care more about the fact that I swore, than that a child has just died.' I was struck to the heart. I knew he was right. So, with over a thousand teenage consciences on the ropes, he came in with a rally call of application for the silent audience: 'I have brought a van with me. Go back to your tents and get anything you're willing to give to the poor.' So, I missed the gig and got my clothes. The sermon had caused a reaction. Maybe even a change in my heart? But the next morning, the main conference leader stood up and essentially apologised for the pressure that had been applied upon us.

Whatever the right or wrong of the approach, it stopped me in my tracks. It made me think: 'Is it possible that we can become so religious that we forget compassion? Is social action really important though? Isn't evangelism the number one thing?' And so, the classic debate began to play out in my heart and in my mind.

Wise words from Wesley

The founder of Methodism in England, John Wesley, has a famous saying: Do all the good you can, by all the means you can, in all the ways you can, in all the places you can, at all the times you can, to all the people you can, as long as ever you can.

What do you think of that? Should the Christian really believe that? I mean, it's not a Bible verse. Jesus didn't say it.

It's not in the Westminster Catechism or a Christian Union doctrinal basis. So, should we really be involved in helping other people? Perhaps we should ask some qualifying questions? For example, should we do all the good we can to all those people? Aren't some people in difficulty because of their own mistakes? Also, what about caring for my own family first? Am I not worse than an unbeliever if I look after someone who doesn't care about their family, at the expense of mine?

Let's be honest, some of us (myself included!), rather than meditating on those words and putting the principle into practice are most interested in discrediting them and justifying why we don't measure up. That wouldn't make us unique or original – let's look at Luke 10:25-37 and Jesus' parable of the Good Samaritan.

Telling you what we all know

You may know the parable well. Jesus was explaining to the gathered audience that the law, the whole law, could be summed up in two commands: Love God and love your neighbour. Which can sound incredibly simple until we begin to ask some more probing questions of ourselves. The scope and the scale of these two instructions often have people wanting to limit their influence and in Luke we have a teacher of the law giving external voice to his internal monologue with the shocking question, 'Who is my neighbour?'

The Good Samaritan is Jesus' response to the teacher's question. You probably heard it in Sunday school or an assembly or two: A man is robbed and attacked – he is in a desperate and destitute situation. But then some religious people came along. But (shock horror) the religious leaders were too busy to care, probably because they thought Temple worship was more important than helping others. Why? They thought the man was dead and could defile them on the way to worship (an Old Testament law stated that you were ceremonially unclean if you touched a dead body). In a nutshell, their religious activity was more important than love.

Jesus wants us to imagine the poor guy on the floor. He'd be lying in his own blood, dazed and confused. Desperate for help. And then he sees a priest – YES! Help has come! But he just walks on by. Doesn't make eye contact. It's the same with the Levite – even though he goes and has a little look – then he walks on too. It must have broken the beaten man's heart and ruined his belief in the God of Israel. Surely these guys would have known the words 'I desire mercy, not sacrifice' from their Bible? Yet, on they walked ... passing by on the other side of the road.

There are often threes in the Bible, and so, as the original audience was listening, they would be waiting for a third person to enter the parable. Possibly the hero of the story? Who did they think that hero would be? Maybe a normal, everyday Jew making the parable an anti-clerical rant? No, the third person was a Samaritan. This would have been a huge shock. The Jews considered Samaritans to be 'mongrels', or, in Harry Potter language, half-bloods.

Just turn back a page to Luke 9:52-54 and see how people thought of them:

> And he sent messengers on ahead, who went into a Samaritan village to get things ready for him; but the people there did not welcome him, because he was heading for Jerusalem. When the disciples James and John saw this, they asked, 'Lord, do you want us to call fire down from heaven to destroy them?'

But look at the quality of the Samaritan's mercy compared to the religious elite: He sees him; he goes to him; he helps him there and then; he takes him to get more help; he leaves money – twenty-four days' worth of food; then he even offers to come back and pay for any more! This is truly generous giving. This goes above and beyond.

The meaning of the parable

Someone has said that when it comes to parables, we need to be willing to walk through the sliding doors. That is, from a distance they are closed. You can see the doors, but nothing more. But just like automatic sliding doors, you need to walk up close for the sensor to pick you up and open the doors to reveal what is behind them. Unfortunately, when you read the New Testament, you see accounts of people hearing the parables, but then just walking away. Never really understanding the true, life-changing, meaning. I wonder, will you go up and let them open – go in?

Let's go through the doors …

The heart of the gospel is about Someone going above and beyond. Remember how Paul put it: 'For you know the grace of our Lord Jesus Christ, that though he was rich, yet for your sake he became poor, so that you through his poverty might become rich' (2 Cor. 8:9). You see, Jesus is the ultimate Good Samaritan. He came to us when we could not save ourselves. He gave Himself for us. And so the argument of the Bible is, because you have been shown mercy, show mercy. As the saying goes: We are saved by faith alone, but that faith does not remain alone.

Remember Ephesians 2? We are saved for good works. And that includes ministries of compassion (sometimes called mercy ministries). Jesus has been incredibly clear that the second greatest commandment is: Love your neighbour as yourself. As He says at the end of the parable, we must all 'go and do likewise'. Let me just spell that out for you. If you love someone as you love yourself, you give them what you think you should have: food; clothing; a dry place to stay; friends; and community.

I know that as Christians we can have pretty different views on social action and helping the poor. I get that. Two books that have helped me in my journey are *Generous Justice,* by the ever-writing Tim Keller, and *When Helping Hurts* by Corbett and Fikkert.[2] In the latter book, there is a helpful early section when the authors give a *tour de force* of the overwhelming biblical call to help the poor. Here are some edited highlights:

- God gives Moses lots of commands to help the poor
- The Sabbath ensures there is rest for slaves and aliens
- The poor were allowed to glean from fields
- Slaves were set free in the year of Jubilee
- Deuteronomy 15:4 says that we should work towards there being no poor
- The prophets repeatedly reveal God warning against worship without mercy
- Acts 4:34 makes 'no needy person among them' as a partial fulfilment of Deuteronomy 15:4
- Throughout the New Testament, care for the poor is a mark of genuine Christianity.

---

2. Tim Keller, *Generous Justice: How God's Grace Makes Us Just* (London: Hodder and Stoughton, 2016) and Steve Corbett and Brian Fikkert, *When Helping Hurts: How to Alleviate Poverty Without Hurting the Poor ... and Yourself* (Chicago Moody Publishers, 2014).

Whatever we think it looks like, it is fair to say that there is a biblical mandate to care for the poor. To have compassion. To be like the Samaritan. But, when it comes to obeying the Bible and Christ in terms of compassion, I find there is one excuse that keeps coming back to me: I don't have the resources. And usually, that means time. In fact, we sometimes don't even see the need to be compassionate, as we don't have time to stop and see the struggling and suffering all around us. Like the teenage me just counting the sermon jokes until the gig, or the religious men on the way to the Temple, we can be so busy that we miss the needs around us.

I wonder, have you ever walked through a city and completely missed a homeless person asking for help because your head was in your phone? Or have you ignored the subtle request for help from a fellow church member because you needed to leave the service in time to take your kids to a birthday party? No? How do you know?! We've probably ignored more people than we would dare to admit. But, I get the feeling that Jesus never did that. In fact, when someone just touched the hem of His garment in the centre of a huge crowd, He noticed them and had time to love them.

Central to this book, as you know, is that sense of being too busy listening to the interruptions of social media and stress that we miss the little Interruptions that could be completely life-changing. Not just for us, but those that God has placed around us. Have we maxed out our lives, time-wise, so that we are too busy to stop and talk to the lonely? Financially, have we committed ourselves to too many direct debits so that we can't give to those who need it when they need it? And emotionally, are we too stretched to be able to care? Dare I ask, have we got compassion fatigue?

I think we need to heed the words of Kent Hughes: 'Love for people, or lack of it, reveals the quality and effectiveness of the philosophy we hold. And from a biblical perspective our love for people is even more revealing, because it actually indicates the authenticity and health of our relationship with God.'[3] Ouch!

We need to live our life in a way that has time for compassion. The gospel of the ultimate Good Samaritan changes everything. This gospel helps us get our priorities right. And we need to be aware of the desire and danger of trying to justify ourselves. Listen to M'Cheyne deal with those of us who want to justify ourselves:

Objection 1. 'My money is my own.' Answer: Christ might have said, 'My blood is my own, my life is my own' ... then where should we have been?

Objection 2. 'The poor are undeserving.' Answer: Christ might have said, 'They are wicked rebels ... shall I lay down my life for these? I will give to the good angels.' But no, he left the ninety-nine, and came after the lost. He gave his blood for the undeserving.

Objection 3. 'The poor may abuse it.' Answer: Christ might have said the same; yea, with far greater truth. Christ knew that thousands would trample his blood under their feet; that most would despise it; that many would make it an excuse for sinning more; yet he gave his own blood.

Oh, my dear Christians! If you would be like Christ, give much, give often, give freely, to the vile and poor, the thankless and the undeserving. Christ is glorious and happy and so will you be. It is not your money I want,

---

3. Kent Hughes, *Preaching the Word: Luke Vol 1* (Wheaton: Crossway, 1998), p. 88.

but your happiness. Remember his own word, 'It is more blessed to give than to receive.'[4]

Triple ouch!

What should I go and do?

It seems to me that the key is to build capacity for compassion into our lives. We need margin in our diaries to have time to help the marginalised. This book is repeatedly coming back to this. It is not about becoming more efficient so that you can do more stuff, rather, it is about learning to say no to certain interruptions, in order to have time for the right Interruptions. And one of those must be compassion.

A book that really got me thinking on this was *Do More Better* by the perpetually blogging Tim Challies.[5] I love the way that he draws the connection between productivity and helping others. Listen to him build his argument. He begins with his foundational claim: 'Productivity is not what will bring purpose to your life, but what will enable you to excel in living out your existing purpose.' This is key and right on the mark with what I am saying. We need to do more to live a full life than just make more time.

So, what is the purpose of life? Challies builds on the foundation: 'The simple fact is, you are not the point of your life. You are not the star of your show. If you live for yourself, your own comfort, your own glory, your own fame, you will miss out on your very purpose. God created you to bring glory to him.' Okay ... but has this to do with helping the poor? Challies continues: 'What are good works? Answer:

---

4. Quoted in: Tim Keller, *Generous Justice* (London: Hodder and Stoughton, 2016).

5. Tim Challies, *Do More Better* (Minneapolis: Cruciform Press, 2015), p.12.

Good works are deeds done for the glory of God and the benefit of other people.'[6]

So, what does that look like?

Firstly, we only see what we want to see. That is, we will only see the opportunities to be 'good Samaritans' when we realise that is what God wants us to be. We need to re-orientate our hearts and minds to be like Jesus and have compassion. We do this by looking at Jesus and loving Him. Think about the initial setup to the parable – it is Jesus explaining the heart of the Bible. For Him, it was simple: love God and (then) love your neighbour. We always love because God loved us first. More than that, we love others in the power of the love that God has for us in Christ Jesus. In fact, even deeper, we love with compassion because the Holy Spirit lives within us and transforms our hearts and minds. So, love God. That is the first step to seeing those who need compassion.

I really want to underline that last paragraph. You see, having reflected on the cow shed swearing sermon, I think I've come to the conclusion that the leader was right to apologise the next morning. The clever clicking of the fingers and the swearing made me do something ... but it didn't change my heart. And that is what we need – a change of heart. The best way to serve the poor is to see Christ. When we see Him, we will become more and more like Him ... the ultimate Good Samaritan. Then we will want to help people in any and every way we can – and that will include eternally through evangelism too.

Secondly, make sure you believe that everyone should be offered mercy and compassion. We are all created in

---

6. Ibid.

the image of God, and Christ died for the undeserving. As such, there are no qualifications for compassion and mercy. By definition those words mean undeserved! And so, every Christian should offer mercy and compassion. This is not an optional extra. If you have been shown mercy, you will show mercy. If you have truly met Jesus – you will meet the needs of others. Jesus told another parable along these lines concerning forgiveness and an ungrateful recipient of a king's mercy. It didn't work out too well for that individual.[7]

Thirdly, as we have seen repeatedly, keep remembering that every decision has an impact. If you fill your calendar too full, you won't have time to stop and help. If you empty your account, you won't have money to give. Pull back and stop over-committing yourself. Don't feel you have to spend all your time and money all the time on status, success and satisfaction. Rather, as Wesley said, realise you can do all the good you can, to all the people you can, all the time you can. Build capacity for compassion.

Finally, this will mean being strategic and sacrificial. There is no easy way to do this. I need to be honest; this will probably hurt. Compassion cannot be done casually. So, build in strategic resources. Make sure you have time to stop. Make sure you have money to give. And be willing to sacrifice. Sometimes, we must give above and beyond what is 'wise'. Remember what the Macedonians described and commended in 2 Corinthians 8:1-3:

> And now, brothers and sisters, we want you to know about the grace that God has given the Macedonian churches. In the midst of a very severe trial, their overflowing joy and

---

7. Matthew 18:21-35.

their extreme poverty welled up in rich generosity. For I testify that they gave as much as they were able, and even beyond their ability.

Wow! What a description! Does that kind of life excite you? Do you want to see instant smiles on those shown mercy, rather than the insta-smiles of social media luvvies? This comes at a price, and it is risky. I'll let M'Cheyne respond to those who say, 'I won't have enough for me': He says that when you say, 'I can't help anyone,' you usually mean, 'I can't help anyone without burdening myself, cutting in to how I live my life.'[8]

That's the bottom line. So, no more self-justifying. Let's listen to the words of Wesley again:

Do all the good you can, by all the means you can, in all the ways you can, in all the places you can, at all the times you can, to all the people you can, as long as ever you can.

At the start of this chapter, I asked if it were possible to become so religious that we forget compassion. Well, the Parable of the Good Samaritan shows us that false religion can allow us to forget compassion. But James tells us something beautiful about it: Religion that God our Father accepts as pure and faultless is this: to look after orphans and widows in their distress and to keep oneself from being polluted by the world.[9] Compassion is truly an essential part of true religion. So, let's make sure we have the capacity to show compassion. Let's be intentional so that we can be Interrupted in the way God intended.

Go and do likewise.

---

8. Tim Keller, *Generous Justice* (London: Hodder and Stoughton, 2016), p. 108.
9. James 1:27.

Selah

1. If you are honest, were you more upset about the preacher swearing, or children starving?

2. What did you think of M'Cheyne's responses to the objections of the 'poor are undeserving'? Do you see how the gospel should fuel our compassion?

3. How could you practically
   'Do all the good you can,
   By all the means you can,
   In all the ways you can,
   In all the places you can,
   At all the times you can,
   To all the people you can,
   As long as ever you can.'?

Prayer

Dear Lord Jesus, Thank You that You stepped down into my world and came to save me, whilst I was still a sinner. You are my ultimate Good Samaritan, as You paid for all my sins, and have made a way that I can live for You, both now and for evermore. Help me to go and do likewise. In your merit I pray, Amen.

8

Communication

After being frisked, asked numerous questions, waiting in line for hours, and then finally climbing the steps to the plane, I got ready to settle into my seat for the next eight hours. I'd been at a leader's conference in one of the fastest growing churches in America, and I was pumped (as they say in the US of A). I was ready to apply all the amazing insights that I had learnt to reach people for Christ.

The plane was full and I sat in the back row with a software engineer. We had a warm conversation about his work, travels and family. He seemed really nice. But then he stopped talking about himself and asked why I was in Seattle. And so, my eight hours of evangelism was about to begin. 'I was here for a Christian conference at a church. I am a minister.'

Before I could get to *two ways to live*, the Roman Road, share my testimony, or draw the bridge illustration on a napkin, he quickly asked the steward to help him change seats! And so, for the next day, I sat quietly on my own, with just my feelings of failure for company.

Have you ever had a conversation like that? Or, to be more accurate, a non-conversation?

Although I am in full-time Christian work and spend my days teaching the Bible, I am not a natural evangelist. I look at people like Glen Scrivener and Rebecca Manley Pippert, and long to be able to start conversations, share Jesus, and see fruit like they do. But often, my conversations are flops. And, more than that, I don't get as many opportunities as them.

One of my heroes is the English evangelist, Roger Carswell. He has an infectious smile and cheeky laugh that he uses winsomely to speak passionately, persuasively and powerfully about Jesus. But what amazes me the most is how he seems constantly to fall into evangelistic conversations. Not just in a mission week or special event, but anywhere and everywhere. I have heard him talk about sharing the gospel with the refuse collectors, someone sitting on a bench, a cold caller and insurance salesman. He just seems to have a constant stream of people to talk to.

Here is a deep theological question: Is this simply down to the fact that our Sovereign God is giving Roger more people to talk to?

Maybe.

Or maybe not.

Whilst it would be dangerous to give a simple answer, I do think that there is a sense in which this is more about obedience to Scripture than a *fait accompli* of providence. I think, within the Sovereignty of God, Roger is following Paul's guidelines for evangelism in Colossians 4:2-6:

Devote yourselves to prayer, being watchful and thankful. And pray for us, too, that God may open a door for our message, so that we may proclaim the mystery of Christ, for which I am in chains. Pray that I may proclaim it clearly, as I should. Be wise in the way you act toward outsiders; make the most of every opportunity. Let your conversation be always full of grace, seasoned with salt, so that you may know how to answer everyone.

Whilst we must be devoted to prayer for open doors, believing that it is God who draws people to Himself, it is also imperative that we 'make the most of every opportunity'. That phrase has the sense of buying every bargain in a January sale. Redeeming the time. Going for it. Not losing out. Being ready.

I don't know the hearts of Glen, Rebecca or Roger, but I would happily bet that they are people of prayer and preparedness. They are always ready.

Planes, trains and authority

God has been teaching me about evangelism for years. From my early attempts at apologetics in my sixth form, to leading mission weeks at universities, running holiday Bible clubs for children, and following up with friends and family, I am always trying to be better at telling people about Jesus.

I remember the first international mission week I went on – to England! I was both nervous and excited as I boarded the train at Swansea and my parents waved me off. Settling at my table seat with all the confidence of a sixteen-year-old, I pulled out my Bible and prayed: 'Okay God, you put someone in front of me and I will convert them!' I was ready to partner with God and help Him out.

As we stopped at Neath, Bridgend, Cardiff and Bristol, loads of people got on the train. The carriage started to fill to capacity. But no one sat opposite me. It was strange. Maybe Satan was too scared to let a poor unbeliever sit with such a potent preacher as me. After a while, we arrived at New

Street Station in Birmingham. I can remember being awed by such a big station underground. And then it happened: a teenager sat in front of me.

I quickly smiled, slipped my Bible into my bag, picked up my Walkman, put on my headphones, and proceeded to have a crisis of faith. My confidence crumbled, my faith failed and my excitement for mission expired.

Two hours later, we pulled into my destination and I awkwardly walked off the train to meet my fellow team members. I introduced myself and tried to put on a brave face. But I had a gnawing fear: how could I be used by God? I was useless. Before we could leave, they explained, we needed to wait for the last team member. And then he arrived, my fellow mission team partner. The guy I had sat opposite on the train!

Straight away, I felt the smile of God. Maybe even the laugh of God. God was teaching me a simple lesson from my slumbering liaison: I could trust Him. He had it all in control.

Looking back at my teenage self, I wonder if I misunderstood the Great Commission. I can remember numerous sermons, talks, conferences and Bible studies that put the emphasis on the word 'Go'. And I loved it! I can even remember preaching a sermon called 'the great adventure'. But in all those talks, the (unintended) message was: *You can do it!* I even wore a Nike baseball cap as my Christian motto 'Just do it'. But, let's be honest, we can't.

As an older Christian with a trail of failures and fears behind me, I have come to read the Great Commission in its entirety. I have finally grasped that the emphasis is on Jesus and not me. The commission starts with Jesus saying 'therefore' and ends with Him promising an 'and'. What are they both? The Great Commission is top and tailed, based upon, flanked, fuelled, and surrounded by the authority of Jesus. He has all authority (He has beaten death on the Cross) and 'therefore' we should go. 'And', more than that, He promises to go with us. All that we do, we do with Him.

Why do we struggle to tell people about Jesus?

I think there are many reasons, but two that affect me are distrust and distractions. I don't trust that God can use me, and I often miss the open doors and opportunities because I am looking elsewhere. As I fill my life with distractions, I probably miss more opportunities than I can imagine.

And so, even though we may have failed attempts like my plane conversation, it is still vital that we place ourselves in a position of action. We need to be able to make the most of every opportunity, even if they seemingly flop. Then, I believe, Jesus will bring divine Interruptions our way. This is the way God wants us to live.

In 1 Peter 3:15 we read these famous words:

> But in your hearts revere Christ as Lord. Always be prepared to give an answer to everyone who asks you to give the reason for the hope that you have. But do this with gentleness and respect.

Evangelism springs up in daily disruptions

As a boy scout I was taught to 'always be prepared.' Life is an adventure and you never know when you might need to dive into a swimming pool in your pyjamas to rescue a rubber brick. Okay, confused? We genuinely prepared for that in school! But, forgetting the silly for a moment, we need to realise that we are constantly surrounded by the possibility of sacred conversations. Significant chats that could see eternity changed.

Peter is clear, we need to be ready for our plans to be disrupted. One of the benefits of limiting the distracting interruptions in our lives is being ready to notice the evangelistic opportunities that come our way. Open doors. There are far more than we realise. When we slow down and pause, stop the rat race, and live life within capacity and with expectancy, I think we will see daily opportunities.

Have you ever noticed how many people interrupted the life and ministry of Jesus? Let me re-phrase that: have you ever noticed how interruptions are the life and ministry of Jesus? He was interrupted by people He didn't know, like the woman with the bleeding and the Samaritan woman by the well. One just saw Him and reached out to touch the hem of His garment. The other tried to avoid Him, but He saw her heart and spoke to her. Jesus never ignored the opportunities because He was catching up on the latest Bethlehem banter or Galilean gossip. He was ready.

But He was also interrupted by people He did know, like Peter and his mother-in-law, and His good friends Mary and Martha. When they were in need, whether close or far away, He was ready to drop His plans and go to see them. His diary had space. Jesus lived a life that meant He was crowded and nearly crushed at times. Yet, by following the rhythms of Sabbath, sleep and *selah*, He had time for interruptions. Those were some of the most important and holy moments of His life.

Do we see daily Interruptions as important and holy?

But, as I have been saying repeatedly, this is not just about being better at planning our diaries. This is a matter of the heart.

Evangelism starts in deep-hearted delight

I am going to keep circling back to this point. If you miss this point, you miss the ultimate point. Peter knew that the best evangelism comes from a heart that reveres Christ. When we know and feel the love of Christ, we will be a people who share the gospel. That is why the final chapter of this book is on communion with Christ. That is the final note I want ringing in our ears. We need to be Interrupted by Him, for Him, to know Him, and draw near.

We can see how this principle works out in so many areas of life. Newly-engaged couples love to tell everyone about their love and lavish wedding plans. Football fans don't have to do a course on 'talking about football' or 'learning ten reasons why your team is the best'. It is an overflow of their obsession. We simply talk about our loves. Everything that comes out of our mouth gushes from the heart.

Ultimately, the aim of evangelism is to take people to Jesus, so we should start there too. If we are with Jesus, we will want others to be too.

Evangelism soars in genuine relational dialogue

Before I explain this point, I need to defend two forms of evangelism: 'cold contact' and 'digital mission'. Both have a place and are used by God. Many people have been brought to the Lord through open-air preaching, literature distribution and talking to strangers on a plane (just not through me!). I am thankful for people who are willing to stand up and speak for Jesus in town centres, army barracks and sporting events.

Reaching out and responding to people online is also a growing and good area of evangelism. Websites and social media platforms are the new church doors and notice boards. Through the Web, we can share the gospel with people from our town or from Tehran. We can answer questions for people who might never be willing or able to walk into a church building. These are wonderful opportunities to make the most of.

Both have their place. And both are hampered by distrust and distractions. Both open-air preachers and online missioners need to have a heart set aflame by Jesus, and a focus that means they can spot opportunities and make the most of them. In his little book, *Digital Dominion*, Jeff Mingee challenges us with this charge: 'You can either mindlessly scroll or missionally engage. But you can't do both.' He then asks the heart-searching question 'Believer, how beautiful is your digital footprint?'[1]

But what interests me in the Peter passage is how he assumes that people will ask you to give a reason for the hope that you have. What?! When did that last happen? When did a non-believer ask you about your faith? This teaching of Peter must surely be the fruit of a life lived in grace. We all know what happened to Peter and how he denied the Lord three times. Yet, in that wonderful beach BBQ conversation, Jesus gives him grace upon grace. Peter's heart was full to the brim with lavish love, and it overflowed.

I would like to call this 'warm contact' evangelism. A sharing of the gospel that happens with people we know and see regularly. Family, friends, neighbours, work mates and baristas. People needed to be up close and personal to see Peter as a man who was loved by God and who loved Him back. It must have come out in his words and actions. More than that, in his attitudes, hopes and fears. He had

---

1. Jeff Mingee *Digital Dominion* (Lancashire: 10ofthose Publishing), p. 92.

a hope that was so deep, people saw it and wanted him to explain it.

As we slow down and savour Christ, and as we live a life of compassion, people will ask questions. They will notice that we don't sacrifice to the idols of success, sex and social media status. They will see us take time to listen, help and talk. We will be different. We will stand out. We will have opportunities. We simply need to enjoy the daily disruptions that can lead to genuine relationship in which we can share the reason for our hope.

I have been profoundly challenged in my thinking on this by Sam Chan. In his excellent book, *How to Talk About Jesus*,[2] Chan is so helpful when he explores the 'plausibility structures' that are needed to help us share the gospel.[3] Surprisingly, those structures aren't good apologetics, funny stories, and powerful testimonies (helpful as they are), but community, experiences and facts. Accordingly, community is the 'most powerful in determining belief'. People need to see a living faith. They need to know a Christian. Then, it is through the lens of that community that people are willing to explore the facts.

Jesus designed the mission of the church to work through Christians in community. That is why the word 'Go' is still important in the Great Commission. It means 'as you go', where you go, wherever you go. In getting on with our day-to-day life, we need to live and speak for Jesus where we are. In a sense, there is no sacred/secular divide. There is no mission/mundane separation. All of life is living out the Great Commission. It's just that most of time we don't realise it and therefore don't make the most of it.

---

2. Sam Chan. *How to Talk About Jesus: Without Being That Guy* (Grand Rapids: Zondervan, 2020).

3. Ibid., pp. 2-3.

We need to be present in community, concentrating on looking for divine Interruptions.

Let's do a thought experiment. Imagine ...

- Walking to school without your air pods in. What conversations could you have?

- Leaving lectures without catching up on TikTok. What comments could you make to friends?

- Having lunch at work without looking at WhatsApp. What chats could you encourage?

- Not rushing on the school run with half-read work emails on your phone. What friendships could you foster?

Let the opportunities be Interrupted

We all have different personalities, gifts and weaknesses. One of mine is speaking. I get paid to preach, teach and meet pastorally with people. This means that I am used to talking and people listening (or looking like they are listening). And so, I have a horrible habit of speaking too much. Way too much! It's probable that you don't have the same weakness as me. But, just in case, let me be clear: We don't wait for someone to ask the question and then proceed to monologue for thirty minutes. That isn't a great idea.

An important part of evangelism is allowing people to interrupt you mid-sentence. That is, make sure it is a dialogue. I can still remember reading *Questioning Evangelism* by Randy Newman[4] for the first time, and

---

4. Randy Newman, *Questioning Evangelism* (Grand Rapids: Kregel Publications, 2017).

realising that Jesus asked questions of people. He wanted to hear them. He wanted to understand them ... or more correctly, He wanted them to understand themselves as they spoke. We need to make sure we let people work through their questions. We need to make sure we let them talk.

I am learning to embrace Interruptions in my life, and I am trying to be ready to make the most of them. Often, it means embracing boredom and not pulling my phone out. Sometimes it means refusing to wear headphones. Neither of those are wrong, but done consistently I am cocooned from the world and the witness I could be.

You may be wondering why I started this chapter with a story about the plane? Surely I was prepared? Surely I was ready to be Interrupted? Yes, I was. I just wanted to start this chapter with a non-starter. Because lots of our interruptions will just fizzle out. But I have learnt to trust God. Not to get discouraged. Just keep going. Keep looking. Keep listening. Keep speaking. Who knows what journey that may have started, or been a part of. Who knows who sat next to him on the next flight? We are responsible for faithfulness, and God is responsible for fruit.

As I finish this chapter, let me tell you about two of the greatest Interruptions in my life. There was the Friday night Christian Union meeting where I went to be encouraged and hang out with my friends. But the preacher went rogue and caused a huge stir. So, I decided to leave my mates and talk to some of the offended. As a result, I met a young guy whom I later had the joy of leading to Christ.

I love my preparation time in the church office, and often get frustrated when someone knocks at the door. But I am so thankful that one lady plucked up the courage to come to my office, share that she wasn't a Christian and ask me to pray with her. Sure, I could have had more time to polish my sermon, but, how much more amazing was it to see someone born again!

I wonder, who will you let Interrupt you this week?

Selah

1. Do you feel like a failure in evangelism? Why?

2. Can you think of times when you might miss gospel opportunities because of your smart phone?

3. How could you use your smart phone and social media for evangelism?

Prayer

Dear Holy Spirit, Help me to devote myself to prayer, being watchful and thankful. Please open doors for the gospel message, and equip me to proclaim it clearly, as I should. I desire to be wise in the way I act towards outsiders, making the most of every opportunity. Let my conversations be always full of grace, seasoned with salt, so that I may know how to answer everyone. In the name of Jesus, Amen.

9

Conscience

I waited in the phone box, not knowing if I wanted someone to answer the call or not. On the one hand, if no one picked up, ignorance is bliss. But on the other, I needed to know. Was she alive or dead? And so, the phone rang, and then the hospital ward nurse picked up. She was still alive, and if I left soon, I could probably make it to be with her when she passed away.

Whilst all of my friends were partying and celebrating the start of their freedom from families in the classic freshers' week chaos, I was about to say farewell to my mother. It wasn't the freedom I was expecting. And so, I made the journey to Singleton Hospital and sat at my mam's bedside as she crossed safely to Canaan's side.

Whilst I was a believer and knew the comfort of the gospel, I struggled with my thoughts and feelings. The pastoral care course in my theology degree taught me about the stages of grief, the importance of talking, and the 'peace we often forfeit' when we don't pray. But there was a problem. I simply didn't like my thoughts.

Unoccupied, my mind would wander to a place of sadness and loss. I would think about things I had said and not said. Of ways I had been a source of pride and pain for my mam. I just couldn't face them. And so, I filled my every moment. I made sure I was never alone with my thoughts.

What's your favourite Pink Floyd song?

One of my coping mechanisms in those days was to play Pink Floyd at full volume. Alone in my room, I could be surrounded by soaring guitar solos and thought-provoking lyrics. But there was one song that had a phrase that kept haunting me: 'Comfortably numb'. No matter how many times I heard that song, I wondered if that described my life. By now, I have come to the conclusion that this is a good way to describe our inner-selves at different seasons and stages. Numb, but comfortably so.

We can numb ourselves in many different ways. Amusing ourselves to death with media like TV, Netflix, books and novels. Even exercise and Strava achievements can help avoid thoughts. Many go for making money, buying things, and getting more stuff. But today, society seems to focus on social media and the internet.

As a result, many of us are hardly ever alone with our thoughts, and therefore seldom deal with deep regrets, hurts, and shame. The 'hopes and fears of all the years' that Jesus came to free us from, are tightly locked away in a box in our mind labelled 'Do not open'. As Earley observes astutely, 'When the distractions fade away and the roar of silence begins, we're confronted.'[1]

We would rather be comfortable than confronted.

For some of us, we have lost the space for conscience, confession, conviction, and therefore a comfort that is deeper than avoidance.

Why has this happened?

---

1. Earley, (Downers Grove: IVP, 2019), p. 73.

The causes of avoidance

It is easy to see how society has encouraged us to fill our moments and minds with medicinal methods. Companies, corporations, and even countries want us to spend money and time. It is good for the economy. They want us to use their products to make us feel better. We even have a term for it: Retail therapy. There is a deeper reason too: Satan. If we delve into our conscience we may find Christ, and Satan doesn't want that. He wants to keep us away from searching our hearts and finding hope.

But, we are not simply victims in this. Let's be honest: we are scared of our conscience, and so we welcome these avoidance tactics. There are numerous reasons for this. For some, we are afraid of crushing condemnation. We fear we are worse than we think and too bad for God. A quiet moment may reveal that there are things in our hearts that we don't want revealed.

I have spent countless hours sitting with people in my church office as they unveil a sin from years ago for which they have not experienced forgiveness. They have buried it and tried to move on. But unforgiven and unprocessed sin, whether done by us or against us, festers, even when unseen. I wonder, have you buried something because you fear God will crush you?

Another reason is the gnawing suspicion that God will give us a boring burden in our times of quiet. It is possible for a Christian to think that God is boring. Or, more accurately, that God's ways (particularly His holy ways) are mundane. We believe that sin is more fun. I have met numerous Christians who think that God will take away anything they enjoy. As a worker with university students, I would often meet someone who didn't want to pray about relationships because they assumed that God would want them to be a single missionary.

But what if conscience was good?

Or, more importantly, what if God was good?

I have come to learn that spending time searching your heart can lead to true comfort. Earlier in the book, I alluded to the first question of the Westminster Catechism, a collection of questions and answers that I value. I have tried to show that our chief end is to glorify God. But I also love the Heidelberg Catechism. And, if I am honest, think that it has a better opening question and answer.

> What is your only comfort in life and death?
> That I am not my own
> but belong with body and soul,
> both in life and in death,
> to my faithful Saviour Jesus Christ.
> He has fully paid for all my sins
> with his precious blood
> and has set me free
> from all the power of the devil.
> He also preserves me in such a way
> that without the will of my heavenly Father not a hair
> can fall from my head
> indeed, all things must work together for my salvation.
> Therefore, by his Holy Spirit he also assures me
> of eternal life
> and makes me heartily willing and ready from now on
> to live for him.[2]

---

2. Quoted in: Kevin DeYoung, *The Good News We Almost Forgot* (Chicago Moody Publishers, 2010).

Jesus is our *only* comfort. He is our true comfort. We shouldn't fear Him, we should flee to Him. What if it worked like this:

Conscience ▶ Conviction ▶ Confession ▶ Consolation ▶ Cleansing at the cross ▶ Close invitation to communion ▶ Comfort (true comfort).

We could be missing out on a key part of true life in Christ if we don't set a course for our conscience.

Not yet Christians: Conviction of sin for conversion

You may be reading this book, and as I have written about Jesus, the gospel, grace, forgiveness and new life, you have realised that you are not yet a Christian. If that is the case, have a little look at Luke 15:11-32 with me:

> Jesus continued: 'There was a man who had two sons. The younger one said to his father, "Father, give me my share of the estate." So he divided his property between them.
>
> 'Not long after that, the younger son got together all he had, set off for a distant country and there squandered his wealth in wild living. After he had spent everything, there was a severe famine in that whole country, and he began to be in need. So he went and hired himself out to a citizen of that country, who sent him to his fields to feed pigs. He longed to fill his stomach with the pods that the pigs were eating, but no one gave him anything.
>
> 'When he came to his senses, he said, "How many of my father's hired servants have food to spare, and here I am starving to death! I will set out and go back to my father and say to him: Father, I have sinned against heaven and against you. I am no longer worthy to be called your

son; make me like one of your hired servants." So he got up and went to his father.

'But while he was still a long way off, his father saw him and was filled with compassion for him; he ran to his son, threw his arms around him and kissed him.

'The son said to him, "Father, I have sinned against heaven and against you. I am no longer worthy to be called your son."

'But the father said to his servants, "Quick! Bring the best robe and put it on him. Put a ring on his finger and sandals on his feet. Bring the fattened calf and kill it. Let's have a feast and celebrate. For this son of mine was dead and is alive again; he was lost and is found." So they began to celebrate.

'Meanwhile, the older son was in the field. When he came near the house, he heard music and dancing. So he called one of the servants and asked him what was going on. "Your brother has come," he replied, "and your father has killed the fattened calf because he has him back safe and sound."

'The older brother became angry and refused to go in. So his father went out and pleaded with him. But he answered his father, "Look! All these years I've been slaving for you and never disobeyed your orders. Yet you never gave me even a young goat so I could celebrate with my friends. But when this son of yours who has squandered your property with prostitutes comes home, you kill the fattened calf for him!"

'"My son," the father said, "you are always with me, and everything I have is yours. But we had to celebrate and be glad, because this brother of yours was dead and is alive again; he was lost and is found.'"

This is one of the greatest passages on conscience and conviction. The son clearly despises his father, as he wants his stuff but not him. In effect, he wants his father dead. He wants to fast forward to inheritance time. There is something wrong with this son, in his heart. And so, he goes to the big city and fills his life with everything. He lives a fast and full life. But then it all goes wrong and he ends up with next to nothing left.

The only thing he is left with is his conscience. Conviction. He knows that what he has done is wrong. Thankfully, he doesn't start scrolling through Facebook, binging on a new boxset, or taking selfies with a filter to hide his true feelings and failures. Rather, he spends time alone, with his conscience. All of his lower-case interruptions and distractions are gone. And then, by the grace of God, he gets a Divine Interruption. He looks at what he has and remembers what he had. The conclusion is clear: His father is better … much better.

The son had been comfortably numb before the pigs. But he was running even then. He had tried to fill himself with anything and everything except his father. The reality is, sometimes we need to be shocked into our conscience. Why? Because we ignore it.

An example of this is the Puritan John Bunyan. Before becoming a Christian and writing one of the greatest books of all time – *The Pilgrim's Progress* – he was far from 'holy'. He filled his life with swearing, playing sports, having fun, and chasing women. But he kept hearing about God. And that didn't sit well. So, he kept pushing God away.

One day he went to church and felt as though the preacher was speaking to him, personally. He went home, ate a meal, and forgot all about it. He stopped himself from being alone with his thoughts and having time for his conscience.

Is that you? Do you need to stop. Slow down. Search your heart? You don't need to be comfortably numb. There is more, much more. There is a comfort in life and death. Going back to Luke 15, did you see what the father did? He ran to the son. He celebrated his return. He gave him everything he had! Dear reader, don't be scared to stop and think. Just remember how the father responds.

Confession is good because God is good

Digging a bit deeper into the parable, it is helpful to understand that the father is not meant to represent God the Father, but God the Son, Jesus. This is because He is the One whom the Father sent for us. Jesus is the One who came to us on that first Christmas morning, gave everything for us on the cross, and ultimately suffered self-humiliation. He became sin and took on our shame, so that we could be the righteousness of God. Right with God.

That could be you too.

Why not join me in a simple prayer that millions have said:

> Dear Lord Jesus, I know that I am a sinner, and I ask for Your forgiveness. I believe You died for my sins and rose from the dead. I turn from my sins and invite You to come into my heart and life. I want to trust and follow You as my Lord and Saviour.

Conscience and the Christian

We must rejoice with Romans 8 when Paul declares *there is now no condemnation for those who are in Christ Jesus.* That is right, there is no condemnation. You cannot lose your salvation. Our union with Christ is assured. But, as I will explore in the next chapter, our communion with

Christ varies. We cannot be condemned, but we can have conviction. There is still a need for conscience, conviction and confession in the Christian life.

Even though we are forgiven, and that is forever, we still need to confess our daily sins. We see that most clearly in the prayer that the Lord Jesus taught us. Have a look at those words that we know so well, Matthew 6:9-13.

Our Father in heaven,
hallowed be your name,
your kingdom come,
your will be done,
on earth as it is in heaven.
Give us today our daily bread.
And forgive us our debts,
as we also have forgiven our debtors.
And lead us not into temptation,
but deliver us from the evil one.

Right at the heart of this most famous of prayers is a request for God to forgive sins. I don't think that is for conversion. We are not saved one day, lost the next, and re-saved the following. No, this is a prayer for the believer to enjoy ongoing communion with the Lord. You can think of it like marriage (which is a picture of the gospel according to Hosea and Paul in Ephesians). Whilst the covenant of marriage remains constant, the experience of marriage will alter. It is similar in the Christian's life (except the covenant will never be broken and Jesus never changes!).

There are sins in the life of the believer that bring clouds between us and God. There are thoughts and actions that grieve the Holy Spirit. And there are patterns and persistent lifestyles that can sear our conscience. But the Lord doesn't want us to box them and move on in a lukewarm state of rebellion. The lack of condemnation does not mean that God doesn't want to deal with the crooked ways in which we are wandering. Jesus wants us to confess them.

We can walk through the Lord's Prayer to see the type of things that Jesus encourages us to expose and repent from. I like to use the Lord's Prayer as an outline and springboard for prayer and confession. A way to see if I am living the way God wants me to. Why not do that now? Stop, selah, and search your heart with these questions.

Our Father in heaven

- Am I living as Your child?
- Am I enjoying Your presence?
- Or have I sought to satisfy myself in other gods?

hallowed be your name,

- Am I living for Your name? Or mine?
- Am I representing Your name well? Witnessing?

your kingdom come,

- Whose kingdom do I want – who is the King of my life?
- Am I building for me?
- Or am I building for, and with, Jesus?

your will be done,on earth as in heaven.

- Am I following Your plan, the Bible?
- Are my decisions based on Your word or my wishes?

Give us today our daily bread.

- Am I trusting You?
- Resting in You for resources?
- Is what You give enough?

Forgive us our sins as we forgive those who sin against us.

- Am I forgiving others?
- Or am I holding a grudge?
- Is there something I am hiding from You?

Lead us not into temptation but deliver us from evil.

- Am I playing with sin?
- Joking around with temptation?

Simply praying the Lord's Prayer slowly – with pauses and questions – searches our heart. Did God Interrupt you then? I hope He did. These are the types of things we can do in the 'boring' times of our days. In fact, these are some of the things we can do as we lie on our beds at night.

The wonderful news is, as we come before the Father, and let our conscience be searched by the Spirit, He will shine His searchlight on the Saviour. The Holy Spirit loves nothing more than showing us Jesus. Thus, when we spend time in our conscience, we will be led to the cross. We see our sin and run to Christ. And there, with the writers of the Heidelberg Catechism, we get consolation, comfort, and confidence that our sins have been forgiven. I love the famous words of John Newton: 'My memory is nearly gone, but I remember two things: that I am a great sinner and that Christ is a great Saviour.'[3] Oh that we would know that more.

Leaving time for Divine Interruptions in our conscience will mean that we will no longer need to be comfortably numb, but can be comfortable in Christ (in life and in death). I love the way Richard Foster put it, 'Confession begins in sorrow, but ends in joy.'[4] So, will you carve out time for your conscience?

Invite the Holy Spirit to search your heart, ask Jesus to forgive your sin, and enjoy the Father's embrace.

Selah

1. Do you find yourself hiding from your conscience?

2. What are you afraid of finding?

3. When you see your sin, do you have a favourite passage you quote to yourself that assures you of God's pardon? What is it?

---

3. Tony Reinke, *Newton on the Christian Life* (Wheaton, Crossway, 2015), p. 49.

4. Richard Foster, *Celebration of Discipline* (London: Hodder and Stoughton, 2000). p. 191.

Prayer

Father God, give me the courage to pray:

Search me, God, and know my heart;
test me and know my anxious thoughts
See if there is any offensive way in me,
and lead me in the way everlasting.[5]

And when I see my sin, help me to trust
Your promise that:

'As high as the heavens are above the earth,
so great is his love for those who fear him;
as far as the east is from the west,
so far has he removed our transgressions
from us.'[6]
Amen

---

5. Psalm 139:23-24.
6. Psalm 103:11-12.

10

Communion

There wasn't a dry eye in the church as the preacher declared 'what God has joined together, let man not separate.' The couple kissed and the congregation cheered. I am sure you have seen that scene many times, and may even have been the bride or groom. It is a wonderful day that celebrates the love that has brought two people together, but also hope for the longevity of their lives together. We all know what happens next: honeymoon together, move in together, live life together.

But what would people think if the bride suddenly went to the door and declared to her husband, 'Thanks for a great day and making me the happiest woman in the world. See you around!' Can you imagine if she then went off to live her own life, in her own home, with her own dreams. You'd be forgiven for wondering if this was a 'marriage of convenience', maybe a way of getting a Green Card or citizenship to a new country.

Could it be that some Christians have done the same with Jesus? We have taken the covenant of our marriage (being joined in union with Christ) but not cherished the outworking of that relationship (our communion with Him through the Spirit). As I started to unpack in the last chapter, Christ not only died to give us union with Him, but also communion with Him. That is, the experience of relationship: Love, peace, joy, comfort, conviction, drawing near, etc.

Before we look at how God wants to Interrupt us with times of communion with Him, I need to make two things very clear. Firstly, communion is the outworking of union. It is because we are united with Christ (and thus indwelt by the Holy Spirit) that we can enjoy communion with Him. Communion is the fruit of union, and not the basis. Secondly, communion is a myriad of different things. These are not just spectacular manifestations of the Spirit. It can be a still small voice, comfort in sorrow, challenge in church, joy in suffering, or assurance amid doubt. Don't limit God or miss out on His wonderous gifts of intimacy.

Creating space for communion
In Chapter 3, we looked at the way in which Jesus would often 'withdraw to a solitary place' (*eremos*). With many of these passages, the word *eremos* is translated in different ways: Remote. Solitary. Desolate. But it was always in order to spend quality time with the Father. The habit has common features: Jesus goes by Himself, often early in the morning, sometimes inviting the disciples to join him, but always to pray.

Richard Foster makes an amazing list of times that Jesus does this:

- Forty days for His inauguration of ministry
- Before He chooses the twelve
- After hearing of the death of John the Baptist
- After feeding 5,000

- After a long night of ministry
- After the twelve have been on a mission trip
- After healing the leper
- On the mount of Transfiguration
- In the Garden of Gethsemane[1]

This withdrawal to be with God was often to prepare for something or to process something. Basically, Jesus dotted His life with silence and solitude – to give it a rhythm. In effect, He was breathing. It is important that we breathe in life. We need breathing space. But that breathing must be more than a Christianised form of yoga; it needs to be breathing space with the Spirit – the breath of God.

The focus of this is not so much on a place as a pace. It is about stepping out and slowing down. Although we can all have our favourite *eremos*, like a mountain, a coffee shop, a chair in the house, or even a layby on the way home from work, the important thing about this is not the location, but the ability to meet with God.

We need to withdraw (silence)
As we have seen, Christians throughout the centuries have spoken about the spiritual discipline of silence. This mainly happens when there is external silence. It is good to find and create quiet places, desolate places. That could be out in creation (like we explored in Chapter 6), by putting a tea towel on your face (like John Wesley's mother), building a prayer closet (a bit extreme), or simply by having a commute without the radio, or walking the dog without a podcast.

---

1. Ibid., p. 122.

Ultimately, we have to turn things off: Social media, entertainment, and work email / phone.

C.S. Lewis imagines how Satan wants to keep us surrounded by noise. In his brilliant book *The Screwtape Letters* he describes how a devil perceives silence and why they want to stop it at all costs: 'Noise – Noise, the grand dynamism, the audible expression of all that is exultant, ruthless and virile – Noise which alone defends us from silly qualms, despairing scruples and impossible desires.'[2] Lewis knew that silence is the soil in which spirituality soars.

But it is not just about quiet on the outside, for you can still have noise inside. There can be a roar of silence. And so, sometimes, we want external noise to drown it out. That's what we thought of in the last chapter. But there is so much more in silence! God wants to meet with us and draw near. And whilst that happens predominantly in church and our devotions, it can also happen in creation, acts of compassion, communicating the gospel and having our conscience cleansed. In all of these, and more, we can enjoy communion with God.

Embrace boredom

We have forgotten how to be bored. Actually, we are scared of being bored. We make sure that every moment of our lives is filled with some sort of entertainment, email or exercise. Not wanting to sound like an old man, but I can remember walking to school with no phone or personal stereo / Walkman / Disk-man / MP3 player / iPod / iPhone (you can see how we have increased our ability to have entertainment at the touch of a screen). In those days, in

---

2. C.S. Lewis, *The Screwtape Letters* (London: Fount Paperback, 1982) p. 113.

allowing my mind to get bored, I actually thought about things. Processed things. Prayed! But now, I always have something to dull the pain of boredom.

The flip side to not having 'boredom' time is that we don't have any time to be Interrupted by God. We don't have moments or minutes for God to nudge us.

A BHAG prayer

The spiritual disciplines of the Christian life have been written about *ad infinitum* over the centuries. I have a collection of 'spiritual classics' in my office that have helped me think through meditation, prayer, fasting, simplicity, solitude and slowing. But I always have a nagging feeling that many of these books come across as a reflective observer's form of legalism. They can be a form of intellectual activism that seeks to commune with God through works. Obviously, I don't believe that is the heart of all the authors. But, over many years of pastoral counselling, I have seen Christian after Christian start to feel like these are exercises that can get you into the presence of God.

Whilst I think all Christians can benefit from learning to read the Bible prayerfully, explore silence and solitude, I also firmly believe that all communion with the Lord is a gift of grace that is only possible through the work of the Spirit. So, whilst God uses means of grace (like church, preaching, Bible reading and the Lord's Supper), we need to look to the Spirit to bring about that experience of communion. Moreover, I think we should pray for it.

Have a listen to Paul:

For this reason I kneel before the Father, from whom every family in heaven and on earth derives its name. I pray that out of his glorious riches he may strengthen you with power through his Spirit in your inner being, so that Christ may dwell in your hearts through faith. And I pray that you, being rooted and established in love, may have power, together with all the Lord's holy people, to grasp how wide and long and high and deep is the love of Christ, and to know this love that surpasses knowledge— that you may be filled to the measure of all the fullness of God.

Now to him who is able to do immeasurably more than all we ask or imagine, according to his power that is at work within us, to him be glory in the church and in Christ Jesus throughout all generations, for ever and ever! Amen (Eph. 3:14-21).

Do you know what a BHAG is? It is an American term that is used in business leadership circles as an acronym for BIG HAIRY AUDACIOUS GOAL. Well, this second prayer in Ephesians is a spiritual Big Hairy Audacious Goal. It is a huge prayer.

Notice the three references to power: verse 16 *strengthen you with power*; verse 18 *may have power*; verse 20 *according to His power*. This is a prayer for power, from power. It is a prayer for power to do 'immeasurably more' than we could ask or imagine. In a nutshell, this prayer is a personal prayer for power, that Christ may dwell in our hearts, and our hearts may delight in Christ's love. When it comes to communion with God, Paul is saying, pray big or go home.

Beginning with the words *'For this reason'*, Paul is looking back to Chapter 3, verse 1, where the flow of argument was broken. The actual context is not chapter 3 but chapters 1 and 2.

There you can read an amazing presentation of the gospel. The glorious grace that is ours through Christ. An awesome Christ-centred gospel that creates a new humanity – the church. So, he's told them that they are one in Christ, and in Chapter 4, he is going to show them how to live as one. But before he does that, he pauses to pray for them. Paul knows that gospel ambitions are powerless without prayer.

Look at how he describes the physical act of prayer: 'Kneel before the Father'. We see desperation and intimacy here. Kneeling was not the usual position for prayer, and isn't in my own non-conformist tradition. But it can be when I am desperate. And look at who he is kneeling in front of … his Father. This is the game changer for our prayer lives.

As a student,I struggled to pray and remember making some public excuses about it in a meeting to an amazing Christian man who bounced with grace and enthusiasm. But in that moment, in front of all my peers, he rightly rebuked me. He told me that Paul wrestled in prayer, and so should I. That had a huge affect on me, and made me want to try harder. But it didn't free me to pray. It didn't give me life. It was only a part of the answer. You see, prayer is not so much about how well you wrestle, but knowing who you are wrestling with.

The real game changer for me was reading *A Praying Life* by Paul Miller.[3] It was like being born again, again. I finally realised that it was our understanding of God as Father that makes prayer a reality. No wonder Jesus taught us to pray, 'Our Father …'

Prayer should be like talking to a father: honest, dependent, open, and natural. This has to be one of the most unique aspects of Christianity – the Fatherhood of God. Looking back at Ephesians 1:5, we read that 'In love he predestined us for adoption to sonship through Jesus Christ,

---

3. Paul Miller, *A Praying Life* (Colorado: Navpress, 2009).

in accordance with his pleasure and will.' As one writer put it, 'God went beyond redemption to adoption.' J.I. Packer wrote, 'To be right with God the judge is a great thing, but to be loved and cared for by God the Father is a greater.'[4]

On the cross, having lived a perfect life, and dying in our place, Jesus obtained: forgiveness of sin; imputation of righteousness; and adoption as sons. It is the full package! **But we need to see that this adoption is not simply external and legal, but relational – communal.** Romans 8 unpacks it:

> For those who are led by the Spirit of God are the children of God. The Spirit you received does not make you slaves, so that you live in fear again; rather, the Spirit you received brought about your adoption to sonship. And by him we cry, 'Abba, Father.' The Spirit himself testifies with our spirit that we are God's children (Rom. 8:14-16).

This is an experience of the Spirit that is for all believers. For me and for you. Understanding this puts us on a journey of expecting more. We don't just want formal externalism. A dry intellectual faith that is simply propositions. I want more than that; I want God … Himself. Isn't that how Jesus described eternal life in His High Priestly Prayer? *Now this is eternal life: that they know you, the only true God, and Jesus Christ, whom you have sent.*[5]

God offers 'immeasurably more' than we imagine, adoption into a relationship. Fatherhood. And our Father God answers our prayers *'out of His glorious riches'*. Not financial wealth – but the gospel. Back in Ephesians 1:6 he defines the riches: *to the praise of his **glorious** grace, which*

---

4. J.I. Packer *Knowing God* (London: Hodder and Stoughton, 1991), p. 231.
5. John 17:3.

he has freely given us in the One he loves. Glorious riches are the glorious gospel of great grace. In chapter 1, we see that we have every spiritual blessing in Christ Jesus – and Paul listed about fourteen of them. It is according to those blessings that we ask this BHAG. If our Father has given us so much, how much more now?!

What does Paul want?

'*So that Chapter 3 verse 17 ...*' The prayer is essentially one request according to Charles Hodge.[6] But with sub parts. So, what does he pray for?

For Christ to dwell in our hearts (*Eph. 3:17a*)

'Dwell' is about living somewhere. Being at home. When you are at home, you belong and change things. You may live in a hotel for a short while (one night or week), but you don't change things. You just complain or move on. Moreover, hotel owners don't let you look everywhere – like the broom cupboard – they are out of limits.

Could this be how we let Christ live in our hearts? He is welcome on a Sunday morning during the worship and Word, but we don't want Him to change things, or search every part. This is not how Christ should be in our hearts by His Spirit. He owns our heart; He has the deeds to the house. He can (and will) change things. He can (and will) go everywhere. But this is a thing of degrees with us. To let Him dwell is to let Him be Lord and become more like Him.

Don Carson comments that this notion is deeply akin to a much-loved emphasis among the Puritans – that *Christ might be formed in believers.*[7] Is Christ at home in your

---

6. Charles Hodge, *Geneva Commentary on Ephesians* (Edinburgh: Banner of Truth, Reprint 1991), p. 124.

7. Don Carson, *A Call to Spiritual Reformation* (Grand Rapids: Baker Academic, 2014), p. 165.

heart? Does He have complete access? As we come to the end of this book I want to invite you to be ready for Divine Interruptions. In helping the poor and sharing the gospel, yes! But also, in knowing and feeling Christ. This is the missing note of modern evangelicalism.

Christ has so much more for us than we realise. The Puritan and theologian John Owen said: 'Our greatest hindrance in the Christian life is not our lack of effort, but our lack of acquaintedness with our privileges.'[8] We need to make sure we know the gospel and grasp God's love for us.

For our hearts to grasp Christ's love *(Eph. 3:17b-19)*

God wants us to know His love. Love is foundational to our faith. We are to be nourished and stabilised by love. How do we know what this love is that Paul is praying about in Ephesians? As every good Bible teacher will tell you: look at the context. In Chapters 1 and 2, he spells out the gospel of grace and shows us the love of God. The Apostle John puts it beautifully in 1 John 3:16, *'This is how we know what love is: Jesus Christ laid down his life for us.'*

Now, what do all these dimensions mean in verse 18? Simple: no matter where you look, there is love. Love is everywhere in the gospel – it is all of love. 'Wide' means it embraces all (Jew and Gentile); 'long' shows it goes into eternity; 'deep' reminds us that it is for the vilest offender; and 'high' helps us see that the gospel lifts us to the heavens. This is a limitless love.

And so, when it comes to verse 18, we need power to grasp it.

---

8. John Owen *Volume 2: Communion with God* (Edinburgh:Banner of Truth, 1998) p. 32.

I can do some simple addition in my mind, but I need a calculator to do divisions and big numbers. But, there are PhD students and engineers who utilise computers to do complex sums. The bigger the number, the more power you need to work it out. Well, according to Paul, we need power to grasp the limitless dimensions of God's love. Divine power! We require limitless power to grasp limitless love!

Just as 'dwelling' is by degrees – so is our knowledge of God's love.

When I married my wife nearly twenty years ago, I knew that she loved me. But, after two decades, I know it *more*. In the same way, we must grow in our understanding and experience of God's love. This is not about something new, but the same love as was shown on the cross. And that love must be known objectively and subjectively. We must understand our union and enjoy our communion. We must never move on from the cross, but we should move deeper into the cross.

And let me underline something here. He is not praying that we would love God more, or that He would love us more. No, he is asking that we would grasp His love more.

Do you believe this is for you?

That you can know God's love more and more?

I believe that in church and conferences, in devotional readings and daily prayer times, in small groups and serving teams, with others and on our own, we can know God more. We can enjoy communion.

In the end, my prayer for you dear reader, is that you would know Christ more. That you would get those distracting interruptions under control so that you can see more Divine Interruptions, and that all of them would ultimately lead you to cherishing Christ.

This is a BHAG prayer.

This is normal Christianity

Before you assume this is not for you, please be assured that communion with Christ is:

- for the new Christian
- the young mum with sleep deprivation
- the businessman with deadlines and debts
- the disillusioned Christian
- the grandmother who has cancer
- the dad or mum trying to balance family, work, church and an elderly relative
- the depressed and stressed
- this is for you.

This is for all of us, as we all have the same Father! In Christ we **all** have a Father who gives according to His glorious gospel of grace! Just in case you missed how amazing your Father is, Paul gives us a doxology in Ephesians 3:20-21. I love the New King James Version (NKJV) here: *'able to do exceedingly abundantly above all that we ask or think, according to the power that works in us'.*

Doesn't this sound more amazing than the latest Twitter trend or work email on a Sunday morning? Wouldn't this give you far more satisfaction than fifty Facebook likes, or reading the newsfeed before breakfast? Can you imagine having moments of communion like this, Interrupting your normal day … dare I say, your boring day? God has so much more for you than the distractions of tech and social media. He has Himself, for you.

Selah

1. Are you scared of silence and solitude? Why do you think that is?

2. Or, are you craving silence and solitude? Why?

3. Where could your *eremos* (solitary place) be? What do you need to do to make that a regular reality?

4. Do you believe that Jesus wants you to know Him more? How does that make you feel?

Prayer

Dear Father in heaven, from whom every family in heaven and on earth derives its name, I pray that out of Your glorious riches You may strengthen me with power through Your Spirit in my inner being, so that Christ may dwell in my heart through faith. And I pray that I, being rooted and established in love, may have power, together with all the Lord's holy people, to grasp how wide and long and high and deep is the love of Christ, and to know this love that surpasses knowledge – that I may be filled to the measure of all the fullness of God. Now to Him who is able to do immeasurably more than all we ask or imagine, according to His power that is at work within us, to Him be glory in the church and in Christ Jesus throughout all generations, for ever and ever! Amen.

Conclusion

Let me end this book with a concession and a confession.

Concession

I know that there are many things that I haven't covered in this book. A lack of time and experience has meant that I've probably missed many of your struggles. There are innumerable ways that we can be distracted or derailed. I just hope I have given you some thoughts on what those might be.

Originally, I had planned to write ten Divine Interruptions, not five. And, as I wrote the book, I thought of many more. I am sure that you can think of other ways that God wants to lead you in paths of righteousness. Could His Divine Interruptions be children, comedy, crying, creativity, classical music or coffee? The point is, I have given you a small selection of what our sweet Saviour can shower upon us when we just open our eyes. Again, I've just tried to whet your appetite.

Confession

All the way through the process of writing this book I have struggled with interruptions. I am uncomfortably aware of the words of Søren Kierkegaard, 'It is absolutely unethical when one is so busy communicating that he forgets to be what he teaches.' I have done that many times over the last thirty months.

But I have been encouraged by an old Puritan. In his wonderful book, *The Bruised Reed*, Richard Sibbs explains how we need to see our sin and be bruised. Oh, how I have been bruised! But then he shows that God won't break us in revealing it. Rather, *'We have this for a foundation truth, that there is more mercy in Christ than sin in us.'*[1]

Grace is glorious.

Dear reader, when you struggle, keep going. Christ is for you.

---

1. Richard Sibbs, *The Bruised Reed*, (Edinburgh:Banner of Truth, 1998), pp. 12-13.

Acknowledgements

It was Wyn Jones, the first elder I served alongside, who drew my attention to the fact that some of Jesus' most important ministry moments were Interruptions. Thank you for helping me put my 'God specs' on. Diolch.

Early parts of this book were read and improved by Sammy Davies, Jonny Raine, Huw Williams, Rebecca Thomas, and Owen Cottom. Thank you for your honesty and wisdom. At times when I felt like giving up, you gave me the courage to plough on. James Sibley was my assistant pastor during much of the writing process. Your friendship, prayers and questions were a source of strength.

A huge thank you to all at Christian Focus. I am still amazed that Willie MacKenzie agreed to publish this book. Thank you for your patience. Also, thank you to Anne Norrie. Your eye for detail and encouraging words made the editing process easy.

Finally, as you can read in this book, I am a man who has often cried *mea culpa*. It is only by the lavish grace of God that I can keep going. And so, I join with all the saints and say, *Soli Deo gloria*.

Christian Focus Publications

Our mission statement –

STAYING FAITHFUL
In dependence upon God we seek to impact the world through literature faithful to His infallible Word, the Bible. Our aim is to ensure that the Lord Jesus Christ is presented as the only hope to obtain forgiveness of sin, live a useful life and look forward to heaven with Him.

Our books are published in four imprints:

CHRISTIAN
FOCUS

Popular works including biographies, commentaries, basic doctrine and Christian living.

CHRISTIAN
HERITAGE

Books representing some of the best material from the rich heritage of the church.

MENTOR

Books written at a level suitable for Bible College and seminary students, pastors, and other serious readers. The imprint includes commentaries, doctrinal studies, examination of current issues and church history.

CF4•K

Children's books for quality Bible teaching and for all age groups: Sunday school curriculum, puzzle and activity books; personal and family devotional titles, biographies and inspirational stories – because you are never too young to know Jesus!

Christian Focus Publications Ltd,
Geanies House, Fearn, Ross-shire,
IV20 1TW, Scotland, United Kingdom.
www.christianfocus.com